ADVENTURE
Story of my life

By
Eva Kiss

Order this book online at www.trafford.com
or email orders@trafford.com

Most Trafford titles are also available at major online book retailers.

Print information available on the last page.

ISBN: 978-1-4120-6600-6 (sc)

Trafford rev. 08/06/2020

 www.trafford.com

North America & international
toll-free: 1 888 232 4444 (USA & Canada)
fax: 812 355 4082

ADVENTURE
Story of my life

Acknowledgement

I would like to thank my husband Laszlo and my two daughters Anita and Csilla for their continued love and support. Also to all the people that have come into my life – both good and bad – I thank you for being part of my life and shaping my experiences over the years.
I would also like to give a special thanks to Helen McKenna who helped me write this book. Without her help, it would never have come alive.

In Memory of Jack
16 January 1993-20 January 2004

Foreword

I would like to give a little insight into what life in Hungary was like under communist rule and why it motivated us to seek a different life elsewhere. I hope it helps to set the scene for the beginning of my story.

At the outbreak of World War II, Hungary hoped to remain neutral, but in 1941 Hungarian troops were sent to join the Germans on the Soviet Front. Hungary then attempted to break away from German control but were unsuccessful. As a result, Germany occupied Hungary in 1944 and later that year the Soviet Union invaded Hungary. The next year Hungary was declared a republic but then the communists gradually gained control of the government, mainly because of the presence of the Soviet Troops in Hungary. The Soviet Union had to resort to military force to impose their regime on the Hungarian people. The communists eliminated all opposition parties and in 1949 they gave Hungary a constitution based on that of the Soviet Union. The head of the communist party ruled the country as a dictator. Hungary was one of seven Eastern European countries that were under the control of Soviet backed communists.

Over time this government almost ruined the economy and created widespread discontent amongst the people. They closed all the borders and set up hidden traps to kill those who attempted to escape.

The entire border between Hungary and Austria was sealed off with barbed wire. They didn't worry about the borders on the Eastern side, because those countries were also under communist rule. You were not allowed to leave the country without official permission and attempting to escape was very dangerous. People from the West were allowed to visit the country and could leave without any problems, but residents did not have the same freedom. If you did manage to escape you could not come back into the country without facing some kind of punishment – this was generally imprisonment as far as I know.

In 1953 Imre Nagy took office as Prime Minister. He had rather liberal views and tried to make some changes, but he was not supported by the Soviets. In 1955 he was forced out of office, but the people had been inspired by the things he had tried to do. In October 1956 all the university students got together and staged a massive revolution, which extended over most of the country. For a few days the revolution was winning and the borders were opened. About 200,000 people left the country during that time, hoping for a better life somewhere else. However, after a few days, Soviet forces were rushed into the country and the uprising was brought to an end. Many people were killed or jailed and many simply disappeared and were never heard of again.

After the revolution the Soviet Union kept Hungary under tight control. They restricted the freedom of the people and you could always feel their presence in everyday life. In primary school and high school it was compulsory to learn the Russian language. The people were brainwashed by the communist party. In the early 1960s things got a bit better, but the Russian Army's presence was still strongly felt. The red star and the Soviet flag were everywhere. In 1968 the government adopted the new economic mechanism 'The Free Market System'. Hungarians enjoyed better personal freedoms than under the communist party, but it wasn't really proper freedom. Those who had left in 1956 were now free to come back into the country without fear of punishment. After the change of government a general amnesty was declared.

Living under communist control meant that there was always general unease within the people. We didn't hear a much about the West but we all thought that things would be better there. Whenever we met westerners they seemed much happier and were free to do whatever they liked without restrictions. We also saw some movies and this showed a different kind of life. Of course with movies you can't be sure what is the truth and what is fiction, but most people believed that life was better outside the Iron Curtain.

One of the restrictions we faced was a lack of choice in things like food, household furnishings and building materials. If someone had enough money to buy a new car, they had to pay upfront, then wait for five or six years to collect a car. We did not have big shopping centres and there was very little private enterprise. The government ran most things - and didn't worry if their customers weren't happy with the service they gave them. This meant that there was no unemployment – but there was also very little incentive for people to go into business because they just couldn't get the supplies they needed. To use food as an example – there was plenty of food available, we did not go hungry, but the choice of food available was very limited. There was hardly any variety. Things like oranges and bananas were only available for a short period in winter and there would be queues that stretched for a kilometre or more because people wanted to get them so badly. But once they ran out that was it and there was nothing you could do about it.

When we left Hungary to go on our holiday we could see that people in Western countries really did have much more freedom in their lives. They could make their own choices and did not have restrictions placed upon them. They just seemed a lot happier and we thought that perhaps we could enjoy a better lifestyle somewhere else. Ultimately that was why we left our homeland. People were shocked when we left. They had no idea we were planning to go and they wondered why we left because we seemed to be doing so well within the context of Hungarian Society. We had a house, a car and a business – these were things that a lot of other people did not have. I guess there was something inside telling us we could live our lives happier somewhere else in the world.

Things have changed a lot since we left Hungary. The fall of the Iron Curtain and the end of communism meant that Hungary became a democratic state. This was good for our family and friends who still live in Hungary and it is nice to know we have the freedom to return for a visit if we want to. Although we had to take quite drastic steps to escape and we had some hardships along the way, we have never regretted our decision to leave and we are very happy with the life that we have made for ourselves here in Australia.

Chapter One

In April 1981 I was 21 years old and living at home with my parents. I had married very young and had a three year old daughter, Anita. My marriage had ended in divorce and I was now bringing Anita up alone. We lived in quite a small village in Hungary – it was very pretty but not very modern. Only the main roads were sealed, the off roads were still dusty and muddy after a good rain. The families lived in brick houses with simple flower and vegetable gardens. Most of the gardens had sheds and people kept one or two pigs and ducks. My parents were without a telephone, even though they had applied for one in 1960, over 20 years before. Our house was very nice; it had three bedrooms and a lovely garden with lots of trees. Our neighbours were friendly people, but like most small towns and villages throughout the world they liked to gossip and everybody seemed to know everybody else's business. My brother lived about 5km away from us. He was married with two daughters, who were about four years apart in age. We used to see each other regularly and were reasonably close.

I hadn't finished high school because I got married and had Anita when I was only 19. However after a couple of years I decided that I would go back to night school and finish my education. I was also working in a construction company at this time, as I wanted to be a building designer and had a talent for it.

Sometimes, an architect would ask me to draw the plans for family homes. He would give me the sketches on a Friday and I would work on them over the weekend. Then he would check the drawings before they were proposed to the council and if there were any problems I would fix them up. This was valuable experience and a good way to learn whilst earning extra money.

The company that I worked for was quite large. I'm not sure exactly how many people worked there, but it was certainly a reasonable number. Every year in April, the company had a huge end of financial year gathering where they thanked us for working hard and told us how productive we had been. Afterwards we had a wonderful dinner and then a big dance. I went to the one the year before and had enjoyed myself, so I decided to go again in 1981. My friend and I dressed up in our best clothes and arrived ready to have a fun night.

The dinner was held in a huge building and there were lots of very long rows of tables that were to be pushed aside when the dancing began. Everybody was very friendly and sociable and I was having a great time. After dinner had finished I looked across at the other rows of tables and noticed a young, really nice looking guy sitting there. At first we just looked at each other. Then we both raised our glasses and said "cheers" across the room. That was it for the moment; we both kept on talking, laughing and drinking with our own friends. The tables were then moved and the dancing began. I was dancing with my friends and work colleagues and really enjoying myself, however, I really wished that my mystery man would come and ask me to dance so we could introduce ourselves. I had never seen him before and didn't know that he worked for the company. I kept on dancing throughout the night hoping that he would come over. I was so happy when he did eventually ask me to dance. I smiled and said, "finally!"

His name was Laszlo and we danced together for a few minutes before he asked me if we could sit down and have a chat. We went over to where his friends were sitting and he introduced me. His friends told me that Laszlo had drunk about six glasses of red wine before he got up the courage to ask me to dance – he didn't like that type of dancing (he preferred discos) and was unsure of himself. He had really wanted to meet me and didn't like the fact that I was dancing with so many other guys. So eventually he took the plunge and came over. We joked about it and had a good laugh, now that the introductions had been made.

We had a great chat and really hit it off. Although it's difficult to explain, both of us felt that we had known each other all our lives. There was an easy familiarity in our conversation and the attraction between us was instant. It was a magical first meeting, Laszlo was so interesting and we never ran out of things to say. We didn't dance again because Laszlo said that he preferred discos and clubs.

I didn't care anyway; I was enjoying his company far too much to worry about dancing anymore. It turned out that Laszlo was a master electrician at the company. The reason that we had never met before was because he spent most of his time working in the capital city about 17 kilometres from where we lived. He was only back at the office about once a month to fill in a report about the work he was doing in the city. After the dance had finished his friends took us back to his parent's house. When we arrived, we picked up his car and he drove me home. I got him to drop me off a few streets away. As I was worried that the neighbours might see us and there would be gossip.

After that first night we met every second day. He wouldn't come to my house; instead we used to meet a couple of streets away so that the neighbourhood gossips wouldn't see us. I was very lucky because Mum looked after Anita for me, so I could go out knowing that she was in good hands and that I didn't have to worry. We usually went to the disco with his friends and enjoyed every moment that we spent together.

The following weekend we went to visit one of Laszlo's friends. I was wearing one of my best outfits and had borrowed my friends white jacket, which was just beautiful. Laszlo had a little blue car called a Trabant and when we were on our way he said that he knew a shortcut that would get us there much faster. So we turned off the main road and he assured me that he knew the road really well. What he didn't realise, however, was that there had been a big storm there recently that had turned the unsealed road into mud! Sure enough we got bogged. At that time I didn't have my license and had never really had any kind of driving lessons. Laszlo said that he would have to steer and I would have to push the car! So I pushed and my friend's lovely white jacket got completely splattered with mud. When pushing didn't work, we had to walk for quite a distance before we could find some timber that we could put under the wheels to give us some traction. Eventually we found some and managed to get ourselves out of the mud. We were very late and very muddy, however. It was definitely a funny way to be introduced to his friends.

The next day they suggested that we go horse riding with them, which I thought was a great idea. I had always loved horses, particularly Palominos – although I had never actually had the opportunity to ride one. I was certainly game to give it a try and was quite excited. When we got to the stables we were told that two of the mares had recently given birth. I rode one of these mares and after we set off I discovered that both of the foals were following me. We were in a very flat area but I was feeling extremely nervous and I'm sure that the horse could sense this. My legs actually started to shake and the horse looked at me with his huge brown eyes as if to say, 'what are you doing?' She then started to graze on the grass, but I was still feeling quite scared. I tried to calm myself by saying 'I can do this'.

The others had all taken off on their ride and I was left alone with two foals and no real idea how to ride a horse! I started to gently kick the horse, hoping that it would make her move. She started to move slowly as if to say, 'I don't know what you are trying to do, but I will follow the others.' When we reached the edge of the forest area she started to graze on the grass again and was just wandering around. I got a bit worried and decided that I would get off the horse before something happened to me. I managed to dismount and led the horses back to the stable area. The people who worked there were surprised to see me and asked if I had fallen off. I explained what had happened and told them that it was my first time riding a horse. They said I should have told them that at the beginning and they would have given me some lessons and a different horse. They gave me another horse and led me into a large fenced area. This was much better for me as they held the rope and gave me basic lessons in horse riding. In the middle of my lessons there was a piercing scream and suddenly everybody was running – I was wondering what was wrong. It turned out that a little piglet had escaped and all the men who worked there were trying to find it. Once again I ended up alone in a field with a horse and not much idea what to do. I decided that that was it; I'd had enough of horse riding! I was actually quite scared and once again dismounted from the horse and took him back. That was the end of horse riding for me! Soon, the others came back having been for a wonderful ride through the forest and past the lake and were wondering what had happened to me! I said that I was never riding a horse again.

After we had met several times, I invited Laszlo to come back to my place. He was a bit hesitant at first, as he didn't know my parents and thought that it might be a bit early to meet them. I then explained to him that I actually had my own house next to my parent's place. When I turned 18 a new rule came in, nobody can own more than one residential property. Because my parents' house was on a double block, mum transferred the vacant block to my name. My first husband and I had started to build a house, but after the divorce it had just stayed the way it was. It was actually a very nice house; but remained unfinished. At that time only the kitchen, bathroom, toilet and one other room were finished. There was a stove as well as my drawing table and a bed, but I never cooked or stayed there – I just used it as a place to work. Laszlo came and stayed there with me that night which was eleven days after we first met and never left! He didn't tell his mother where he was – he just went to and from work from my place. After several weeks he asked his mother why she hadn't been worried about where he was. She replied that she knew he must have been OK wherever he was staying, or else he would have come back home again. She really was so sweet; I love both his parents dearly. The way he met my parents was actually quite a funny story. The stove wasn't working and he was trying to fix it. He was wearing old clothes and had grease all over his hands and arms. I didn't have anything that he could clean the grease off with so I suggested we go and see my mother. Laszlo was introduced to my parents in his old clothes and with grease all over him! They were a bit surprised at first, but they really liked him right from the start. They thought he seemed like a decent guy and were very impressed that he could fix things and didn't mind getting dirty.

Things were going well in our new life together. We went out to the disco most weekends as we both loved to dance. We also started building up the house slowly but surely. Laszlo brought a fridge to the house & had a hot water system installed and things seemed more permanent. It felt so natural for him to be living there with me while we completed the house together. It felt like we had been together for much longer than we actually had. We gradually finished off the rest of the rooms, doing things like painting, putting up wallpapers, carpet and vinyl in our spare time.

After we had been together for a few months, Laszlo decided that he would like to set up his own business as he wasn't very happy with his job at the building company. He obtained the necessary licences and permits and set up on his own. I still had another year left to complete my schooling so I decided that I would go back in September. Towards the end of 1981, Laszlo asked me if I would like to have another baby. At first I replied that I didn't think so. I didn't really want to be pregnant again and I thought that one child was enough for now. But I told him I would think about it as I could see that he really wanted to have a baby with me. I eventually decided that I would like to have another baby and we went to visit the doctor. He advised me that I should come off the pill and wait at least two months before trying to conceive, in order to allow my system to clear. Coincidentally the two months was up on the 14th of February, although at that time we had no knowledge of Valentine's Day. It wasn't an occasion that was celebrated in Hungary. Very soon afterwards I had some slight bleeding and I said to Laszlo that I was pregnant. He didn't believe me – we had only just begun trying for a baby and he didn't think that I could possibly know so soon. But I told him the same thing had happened when I was having Anita and I just knew that I was pregnant again. Sure enough a few weeks later I went to the doctor and he confirmed it. I guess I was very lucky to get pregnant so easily but on the other hand I had to be very careful in the future.

The pregnancy wasn't too bad, I did my schoolwork and things went on normally for a while. One day I asked Laszlo if he wanted to marry me seeing that we were living together and were having a child together. He replied that he definitely wanted to marry me and we started making plans there and then. We decided that the anniversary of our first meeting – the 24th of April – should be the date. Fortunately it fell on a Saturday. It was only a small wedding with close friends and family. That was held in a really nice restaurant in a big hotel. We had a lovely dinner after the ceremony and a wonderful evening. Anita was almost four at the time and she had a great day as well, although she was very tired soon after the dinner. The waiters put some chairs together so she could lie down and sleep. They offered to tuck her in but she said that she wanted her Mummy. So they asked her which person was her mother and she replied in quite a matter of a fact way, "The bride is my mother of course!" The waiters were a bit surprised but they came and found me and I tucked her in so she could sleep. All in all it was a beautiful and memorable wedding.

Laszlo did professional judo a few times per week. He also used to teach children once a week at night and on weekends as well as competing in some competitions – so all in all it was very important to him. I found it quite interesting to observe that he was such a sporty type and there I was, never really doing any sports at all. I sometimes used to wonder why Laszlo was attracted to me when he was so muscular and fit and I wasn't. But I knew that it didn't matter to him and that he loved me just as I was. The main thing was that he really enjoyed his judo and had a lot of fun.

We didn't have much contact with my first husband. He was supposed to take Anita every few weekends, but most of the time he didn't show up. When he did come, Anita would often complain that they had gone to the pub and his friends were drunk and that she didn't like it. Eventually his visits stopped; unfortunately he just didn't seem very interested in spending time with Anita.

I seemed to grow quite fast with my second pregnancy and by five months I had quite a tummy. At first they thought that I might be having twins. My Dad is a twin and Laszlo's mother was also a twin. Ultrasound scans weren't really available then, but later in the pregnancy they checked the heartbeat and confirmed that there was only one baby after all. Laszlo often got extra jobs doing stunt work, because of his judo expertise. He even appeared in quite a few movies. On one particular night he arrived home very late and to save me from going downstairs he climbed up the scaffolding outside (the house was rendered by the builder) and knocked on the balcony door – it was like a scene from Romeo and Juliet! However I was half asleep and hearing his voice I automatically went downstairs to let him in. I couldn't work out what was going on when I opened the door and he wasn't there. It wasn't until he called out again that I realised where he was.

By the end of my pregnancy my legs were very sore due to varicose veins. I couldn't work in the last stages because of my painful legs, but I did finish my study to allow me to become a designer. I was very happy when I received my certificate that allowed me to design and draft family homes. After the baby was born and things had settled down again I planned to work from home. This would allow me to look after the children but also to use my skills. Our baby was due on the 22nd of November.

When Anita was born, it was past my due date. The umbilical cord had been wrapped around her neck and she was almost blue. The doctor was a bit concerned that this might happen again and he said that I would be induced if I hadn't gone into labour by the due date. So on the 22nd of November I went to the hospital early in the morning to be induced. They gave me the drugs but nothing happened for a while. At about 12 o'clock I told the nurses that I thought the baby might be coming. They didn't believe me at first, but I convinced them that something was happening and they examined me. They agreed that things were moving but the birth was still quite a while away. I disagreed and told them that I felt like I had to push. They took me into a room with two beds that I remembered from when I had Anita. When she was born I had been on the left bed. I was hoping for a boy this time so I said that I had to go on the right bed, otherwise I would have another girl. The nurses told me I was being silly and that I had to go on the left bed. They called the doctor to come urgently and very soon afterwards our daughter Csilla was born. I had a little laugh and said to the nurses that I told them I would have a girl!

My mother had rung just as the head was emerging. The nurses told her that the baby was almost born but they couldn't say what sex it was yet. So she had to wait for a few minutes and ring back again. It was very nerve wracking for her. She was relieved when she rang back and found out that she had another granddaughter and that everything was fine. Laszlo had been with me at the hospital in the morning. Nothing was happening at that time so he had gone home only to be told by Mum that the baby had been born. He couldn't believe it had happened so fast and he then came back to the hospital and met his daughter when she was an hour old. Afterwards he went home and smoked a lot of cigarettes (he used to smoke occasionally but not too much because of his sports). He also drank a bottle of Napoleon Cognac and danced all night. The next day he gave up smoking altogether.

I was in hospital for about five days after the birth. Everything was fine and both Csilla and I were healthy. When we first bought her home Laszlo was a very nervous new father. He checked Csilla every few minutes to make sure that she was OK. He was also very excited that we had our own little daughter. Anita was a very good baby but she had cried a lot at night and I didn't want the same thing to happen this time. So we let Csilla cry during the night (after checking that she was OK) so that she would learn to sleep by herself. After four days she would sleep from her 10pm feed until about 6am the next morning. All in all she was a very good baby and we didn't have any problems with her. Anita was about four and a half when her little sister was born and she loved her right from the start. I couldn't have wished for a better big sister for her. She really looked after Csilla and was always checking on her. She always used to ask me when she was going to grow up a bit so that they could really play together. Anita also loved Laszlo like a real father, maybe even more than her real father. Even these days she considers Laszlo to be her father. The very first time she met him she said, "You are a cheeky boy" and from that moment on they got on really well. He always loved Anita as well and treated her as his own. After Csilla was born he never treated them any differently.

Soon Csilla started to grow and change quickly, like all babies do. I breastfed both girls until they were nine months, which was a very happy experience for me. As Csilla started to get a bit bigger I started my design and drafting business from home. I was lucky because my Mum worked for the council and she could refer people to me who wanted to build a home and needed a designer/drafter. I started slowly but gradually established myself. Laszlo's business was going really well too, although he had many problems getting the necessary materials for his jobs. At that time in Hungary it was very difficult to get most materials. You had to know somebody who could pull some strings and even then you couldn't be guaranteed of getting what you wanted. For this reason it was almost impossible to meet a deadline. Laszlo was always proud when he and his workers met their deadlines, but sometimes it was with great difficulty. At times I would have to go and get materials or we would almost have to bribe people to get what we needed. Ordering things didn't necessarily mean that you would receive what you needed; sometimes the required materials were just not in the country. It wasn't just building materials either. Even things like curtains and other household goods were very hard to come by. It was very difficult to decorate and furnish a home properly. There were many things that you just couldn't buy at all and it was very frustrating. Things were also very expensive. We just went along day by day but even so, we knew that we were better off than many other people. At least we had our own home and car and Laszlo had a successful business and I was also doing quite well.

When I was designing houses I had to take photos of the surrounding houses so that the council could judge whether or not the house would fit in. The problem was that I only needed to take about two photos at a time but all rolls of film were for 24 shots. So it was very expensive and wasteful at times. One day Laszlo gave me a surprise and got me a Polaroid camera. It was definitely much more practical for what I needed. He had bought the camera second hand at a pawnbrokers shop and had paid quite a lot of money for it. However when he went to buy a film cassette at a camera shop, they told him that they weren't sold in Hungary. So he then went back to the pawnbrokers shop and told them that they had sold him an expensive camera that he couldn't use in Hungary because he couldn't buy the film cassettes. They were unsympathetic and told him that it was his problem. He asked them how they could justify selling him and unusable product. He was very upset and frustrated that he had bought the camera for me to make my job easier and now it had been a big waste of money. I was also very angry and decided to write into a popular magazine, explaining the problem that we had come across and expressing our frustration with the situation. I didn't even think my letter would be published, so I was very surprised when it was. I was also amazed to receive many letters from all over Hungary – many of them were from shops that had one or two cassettes left and offered them to me. The most amazing response, however, came from outside Hungary. I received two packages in the mail – one form West Germany and one from Norway. Both of them contained a lovely letter and a cassette. I was really touched that people who lived so far away had gone to the trouble and expense of buying me a cassette and sending it over. These people were Hungarian and although they were living in Western Europe they still subscribed to this Hungarian magazine. This experience showed me that there were many kind people in the word who were willing to do a good deed for a stranger. I wrote back to the people who had written to me and in the process made some lovely new friends.

When Csilla was between six and eight months old I noticed that she wasn't gaining weight at all and I was quite concerned. I knew from Anita that babies grow very fast in the first year, but even though Csilla was feeding well she wasn't growing out of her clothes at all and was just not gaining any weight. I took her to the doctor to see if something was wrong as she also had a slight fever as well. The doctor checked her over and said that there was nothing to worry about. She said that seeing as Laszlo and I were quite small; it was only natural that our child was small as well. I wasn't happy with this diagnosis however and took Csilla to a middle-aged doctor, who knew our family well. He examined Csilla and said to me, "I honestly don't know what is wrong with her but it definitely isn't normal that she isn't gaining weight. Take her to get some blood tests done and bring the results back to me".

Getting the blood tests done was very traumatic, because Csilla was so tiny. Doctors found it very difficult to find a vein in her arm. After several unsuccessful attempts on both arms I was getting very upset and poor Csilla was screaming. I asked them to stop and to get somebody who knew what they were doing. Fortunately another nurse came in who knew what to do and the ordeal was over in minutes. We had the blood tests done in the morning and took them back to the doctor in the afternoon. He looked at the results and said, "Oh my God, take her straight to the hospital". He still didn't know exactly what was wrong but he could tell by the tests that something was definitely not right as certain levels in her blood count were too high or too low.

After five days in hospital they checked everything and finally did a faecal sample and discovered that she had Giardia Lumbia. It was a type of intestinal parasite that was eating all the food that Csilla was ingesting, which explained why she wasn't growing. It was only tiny but could multiply fast. Being a very serious illness the doctor said that without treatment she could have died within four or five months. It was extremely lucky that the second doctor had listened to my concerns and had the tests done. After the diagnosis was made, Csilla was given the necessary medication and she made a full recovery, which was such a relief. Because of the delay in her growth, we had to take her to the doctor on a regular basis so that they could monitor her progress. They would regularly x-ray her left arm to check on her bone growth as well. The doctors said that it would take about 10 years for her to catch up on her physical growth and we did notice that she was behind kids her age in height and weight. But it hadn't affected her brain or intelligence in any way; she was just a small child.

Living next door to my parents was very hard sometimes. We ran our own little household very well, but my mother loved to be 'helpful'. I appreciated her help but sometimes I felt a bit smothered because I wanted to do things my own way. By trying to be helpful she would try and run our household as well as her own. She would often bring food to us, which wasn't so bad, except I didn't know when she was going to do it. Many times I would have already cooked our own meal and she would then bring something over, so we would end up with too much food. At times my Grandma would also bring something to us as she lived with my parents. It was uncomfortable when they bought food over that we didn't need. On one occasion Mum brought us chicken soup and I said to her that while I appreciated her cooking for us, we wouldn't be able to eat it because I had already cooked our meal for that night. I also said that we could run our own house and that we would be OK, so she didn't have to worry about us at all. My mother then replied that I couldn't cook or clean properly so one day we would either starve or the dirt would eat us! I have never forgotten that sentence and I still think about it even now. Sure I hadn't done much cooking when I was younger and living at home but that was because it was all done for me. But everybody has to learn and I considered myself to be a better cook than my mother anyway! We always ate well and my house was always clean. So it was very hurtful to hear those nasty and untrue words. After this conversation my mother didn't say anything else, she just picked up the soup and walked out the door.

When Laszlo came home a bit later, he asked me what that stuff was spilt on our verandah. I didn't know what he was talking about so I went to have a look. It was chicken soup! Mum had obviously been so angry that she had thrown it on the front door as she left. Laszlo was quite annoyed and he actually went over to see my parents and said that this situation had to stop. He explained that while we appreciated the help that had been given to us, we were married and would like to run our own lives. He also said that if we needed help we would ask for it.

Chapter Two

When Csilla was about one, the man from
Norway asked if we would like to come and
visit him. I thanked him for the offer but didn't
think it would be possible. However I decided
that we should at least give it a try and hope for
the best. At that time in Hungary you could
only go to Western European countries such as
France, West Germany or Norway once every
three years. For entry into these countries you

were required to have a blue passport. You had to apply for this passport and a special visa and your trip had to be approved by the government - you couldn't just pack up and go on a trip there. You were lucky if you gained approval. To go into Eastern European countries such as Romania, Yugoslavia or Czechoslovakia it was a different matter. For these countries you required a red passport and you could go there whenever you chose. Another factor about going into Western countries was that you could only change a very minimal amount of money. It was very limiting and didn't give you an opportunity to do anything very expensive. We had to apply for our blue passports and hope for the best. I went to America with my mum, when I was 11 and once to West Germany when I was 17. Every time you needed to apply for a new passport. Laszlo had a red passport as he had travelled to some of the eastern countries for judo competitions. I also had to gain approval from my first husband to take Anita with us. At first he wasn't very keen on the idea. But eventually he agreed to sign the papers.

We were very happy when our blue passports were approved and we could plan our trip. We had to pay for a visa into Austria, West Germany and Norway but they said that we didn't need one for Denmark – where we had to catch our ferry to Norway. We had booked and paid for our ferry trip before we left home because of the limited amount of foreign currency that we were allowed to take with us. In June 1984 we set off on our trip. We now had a Lada, which was a pretty good car, but it wasn't in great condition. When we passed through the border from Hungary to Austria we were checked out very thoroughly. We had to get out of the car and they checked our height, hair and eye colour to make sure it matched our physical descriptions. So we were quite surprised when we got to the German border and it was much more relaxed. We stayed in the car and they just took our passports and stamped them and then waved us through.

Our first stop was to visit our friend in Munich who had sent us the cassette for the camera. We had an enjoyable few days with him, he was very hospitable and showed us around his city. Next we visited my uncle and his family who also lived in West Germany, in a town called Ludwigshafen. Unfortunately this wasn't such a great experience. We asked my uncle if we could perhaps borrow some West German currency so that we could have some more spending money and said we would pay him back in our currency the next time he visited. He said that if we didn't have enough money then we shouldn't have been taking the trip! Despite this they insisted that we come back and visit them again on our way home. So we marked a date on the calendar when we would be coming back, even though we weren't that keen on seeing them again. However we thought we should do it to be polite to our relatives. The drive through West Germany was a very long day and we travelled almost 1100km. Because West Germany didn't have speed limits on its autobahns, we averaged about 130 or 140km per hour, which allowed us to cover a lot of ground. As we drove along, Csilla decided that she would hold Laszlo's hand as he drove. She then put her hands on his face and turned his head around and said, "I love you Daddy!" Laszlo replied, "I love you too, but just don't do this to me while I'm driving at 130km per hour!" It was very sweet all the same.

After leaving West Germany we drove through Denmark so that we could get to the town where we had to catch the ferry. When we crossed over the border the guards asked us where our visas were and we tried to explain that we were told that wasn't necessary. It was a bit stressful because they asked us to get out of the car and then took us into an office. We had heard bad stories about Western border crossings. The guard asked for our names and dates of birth and checked our descriptions against our passports and stamped a visa. I asked him how much we had to pay but he said not to worry about it. He told us to have a good trip and that he would see us on the way back.

We eventually found a little motel where we could stay the night. Because we only spoke Hungarian, communicating in Denmark was a bit difficult. We worked out that one of the meals was included in the price but we weren't sure if it was breakfast or dinner. After sitting in the restaurant for a while we were wondering why nobody came to serve us and also why were hardly any people there. Eventually we managed to work out that it was breakfast that was our included meal, not dinner. So we went back to our room and had a good nights sleep after our long drive. In the morning we made sure that we had our free breakfast. The ferry was due to leave at 11am and we allowed ourselves plenty of time to get there. When we arrived it was quite strange that there were hardly any other cars or people around. It was just a tiny fishing village but we felt sure that there would be many more people waiting to catch the ferry. As the time got closer and there was nobody else around we finally saw a woman and managed to ask her where the ferry was. She explained that it had left at 8am. We couldn't believe it, but she showed us the timetable and she was correct. So then we showed her that we had booked and paid for our trip and that the time of departure was shown as 11am. She then worked out that the departure time we had was for June and it was now July. Apparently the travel agent at home had made a mistake. We were in a bit of a fix. We had hardly any money left and the price that we would have to pay here was almost double what we had paid in Hungary. Still, we wanted to go to Norway so we decided to pay the extra money and wait for the next ferry, which was at 11pm that night meaning we had to spend the whole day in this tiny little village.

It was a cute little place and we enjoyed wandering around, but it was a long time to spend in such a small place, especially when we didn't speak the language. It was also very hot. We were extremely bored by the time night came around and couldn't wait for the ferry to arrive. We asked Csilla how big the ferry was and she opened her arms and said, "Ooooh, big!"

She was so cute, but it was such a long day for her. Anita looked after her well but she was also very tired by the end of the day. It was such a relief when the ferry finally came and we were awed by the size of it. We had never seen anything like it in our lives! It had five levels of car parking and then had the same height in cabins and sitting levels. We could only afford to have seats, but they were reasonably comfortable and we thought we would be able to get some sleep. Laszlo always likes to explore so he took Csilla to have a look around the ferry. When he came back a short time later, Csilla was no longer with him. I panicked for a moment and wondered what could have happened to her. But instead Laszlo said, "come and have a look at what we found". It turned out that they had discovered a huge playground that had a Lego land and many other toys. I ran back with

Laszlo to see Csilla playing happily with the other kids. She was tiny but she was still a normal little girl who loved to play. She was even pushing the other kids out of the way so that she could have extra turns on the slippery slide. Everybody was looking at her because she may have been tiny but she was pushing all the other kids around! She was surprisingly strong for her size and wanted to be first. She was having a great time and I was reluctant to leave but I had to go back to Anita, who was minding the bags.

Anita and I ended up sleeping on the seats, which weren't particularly comfortable. Laszlo and Csilla ended up sleeping in the car. This wasn't allowed, but nobody checked so they stayed there and had a better sleep than we did. We were just drifting off to sleep when Anita told me that she was feeling sick. It was windy and quite rough and you could really feel the motion of the ferry going up, up, up and down, down, down. It was hard on the stomach but it would have been very difficult to manage if

Anita had been sick. I didn't know where the first aid area was or even how to speak the language. So I said to her to try and breathe deeply, relax and go back to sleep. Luckily this worked and she was fine for the rest of the night. We ended up arriving in Norway at about 7am and knew that we had about 300km of driving ahead of us.

When we got off the ferry we assumed that there would be some kind of border crossing to have our passports checked, but there was nothing at all. It was a tiny little place and there was nobody around. So we just drove off and eventually came to a freeway with a tollgate. Neither of us had ever seen a tollgate before and we didn't have a clue what we were supposed to do. There was also nobody around to ask or even to watch what to do. We just didn't know how we were supposed to get through! After seeing a money sign on the basket we used some logic and Laszlo came up with the idea that maybe we should throw the money into the basket. We gave it a try and were so relieved when it worked! We felt a bit silly afterwards and had a good laugh about it. We then drove through Norway until we reached our friend's place in Brumunddal.

It was the second week in July when we arrived. Our friends were wonderful people and very hospitable and they had a nice little home. Everybody was quite surprised that we had chosen to come to Norway on our summer holiday because it was such a cold country. In any case it turned out that Norway's best two weeks of summer weather was the time that we were there. Most of the factories and other workplaces were closed down for two weeks, as it was the time that most Norwegians took their summer holidays. Lots of people had gone off in their motor homes or caravans. We were already aware of that because our friend had told us. He was retired but he took us to the factory that he used to work at and introduced us to the people who were servicing the machines. He was very proud to have us visiting him and told everybody that Laszlo was an electrician who worked for himself.

The people that we met were all really friendly and we felt very welcome.

The countryside in Norway was beautiful. There were lots of trees and forests and everything was very green. There was also fresh, clean water from the mountains. Amazingly the grass and soil was still cold to sit on even though it was summer. The weather was very warm (between 25 and 30C°) but the ground was still cold, which was quite amazing. We took the kids to the lake and to a water fun park and all in all had a great time. We also saw a lot of display homes. This was quite new to us, because you never saw anything like that in Hungary. It was very interesting to me as a designer. In Hungary our homes were built of brick and they had thick walls, double-glazing, heating and a roof pitch of about 45°, to cope with the snowfall. Norway was almost 2000 km north of Hungary and was much colder on average. It regularly had snowfalls between one and one and half metres deep and the temperatures could be as cold as -35C°. However their houses were made of timber, which was a real surprise. They had 200mm insulation all over the house, including the ceilings and the walls. They had triple glazing on all their windows and the pitch on their roofs was only about 25-30°. They actually went up on their roofs and cleared the snow away themselves, so it wouldn't fall to the ground and injure somebody. It was very interesting to note the differences in their architecture. Their homes were like kit homes but were beautifully finished and they made their basements out of besser blocks.

Staying in Norway was a wonderful experience for our whole family. The two weeks passed by too quickly and it was hard to say goodbye when the time came to go home again. We didn't catch the same ferry back as we had come via Oslo this time and thus crossed the sea in a different place. This ferry was much smaller and it didn't seem possible that it would make it across with so much cargo. But it did, of course and I was quite amazed when they managed to turn the ferry around so easily when we docked on the other side. It had been a long and boring day on board the ferry but eventually we arrived back in Denmark. Once again there was no border crossing to have our passports checked. So in actual fact we didn't have any stamps in our passports to show that we had even been to Norway at all.

We headed back to my uncle's place in West Germany. That night we slept on the side of the road because our money was getting quite tight by this stage and we only really had enough for petrol and food. We arrived back in Ludwigshafen and found my uncle's house easily enough. However when we knocked we soon realised that there was nobody home. This wasn't a very nice situation to be in so we went to a nearby park to work out what we should do. We decided to eat our sandwiches, but we discovered that the cheese was mouldy and had to throw them away. Nothing was going right! We didn't really know what we were going to do. We didn't have enough money for accommodation, hardly enough for food and just enough for petrol and now we found that my uncle wasn't home. I did remember, however, that when we had visited when I was about 17 we had gone to see my uncle's wife's family, who lived nearby. The problem was I didn't know exactly where they lived. But we were in a desperate situation so I thought about it really hard and figured out where we had to go.

Amazingly enough we actually found the place and decided to go and ring the bell. It was the right house, which was a huge relief. The only problem we had was with the language. They didn't speak any Hungarian and we didn't speak German. It was certainly an interesting experience to try and explain what had happened. We did our best with sign language and hand signals and they understood what we were trying to say. It turned out that my uncle and his family had gone on a holiday. We found this really strange when they knew when we were coming back and also because they had insisted that we visit them again, even though we weren't that keen on the idea ourselves. In any case they did understand our predicament and said that we could stay with them for a couple of days, which was very kind – they were really nice people.

After we had been there for a little while, they remembered that the couple who ran the bakery nearby were Hungarian. They took us to the bakery and we could then translate our conversations properly. These people were very kind to us as well. They filled two bags with delicious bakery food for us and refused to take any money. We were very touched by their generosity. My uncle's in-laws then rang my uncle to find out what was going on. He didn't seem very concerned about what had happened and said that they wouldn't be back for a couple of days as their holiday wasn't over. We couldn't believe it – everybody was being so friendly and helpful except for my uncle!

After a couple of days my uncle returned from his holiday and seemed quite surprised that we had come back to visit him again. I reminded him how he had insisted that we visit and also how we had marked the date on the calendar and let him know that we didn't understand why he had put us in that position. This was our second uncomfortable experience with him, but he didn't seem to realise it. We stayed for one night and then I said to Laszlo that I wanted to leave. I didn't care if we offended my relatives or not but I just couldn't stand it any more. Amazingly my uncle then tried to get us to extend our visas and stay longer. He said that they really enjoyed having us! We declined and left as soon as we could.

Before we left West Germany we went to stay with our friend in Munich again. We had a good look around the city and had a great time. Before we left, our friend had some of his friends over for dinner and during the conversation they asked if we would like to stay in West Germany. At first we didn't know what they meant and in any case we weren't even sure if it was possible. They then explained that if we wanted to we could go to this particular place and apply for residency. It was an interesting idea but we didn't consider it seriously at the time. We explained that we had a home and a business back in Hungary and were quite happy to go back home. We had had a great trip but it was just a holiday and Hungary was home. We really didn't take the offer seriously at all and didn't speak about it again on the trip home. After we left West Germany it was a long trip home, but we made it OK without running out of money. Something wonderful that happened on this trip was that Anita started calling Laszlo 'Dad' – something she had done ever since.

All in all, the entire trip was a very happy and positive experience for the four of us, making our little family unit feel much closer.

When we arrived back home only my Grandma was there, but we soon settled back in and got our normal life organised again. However we were still having problems with my mother being overly 'helpful'. No matter how many times we told her that we wanted to learn from our own mistakes, she would still try to run our finances and even our normal day to day life. We were uncomfortable with this and eventually Laszlo and I decided that we needed to sell the house and move somewhere that was further away so we could be more independent. I didn't like being angry with my mother all the time, but it would keep happening if we stayed so close. I knew that her intentions were good but she would just take over and start controlling everything. Some people are comfortable with this but not us. We just wanted her to be there when we needed support, not all the time.

After being home for a few weeks we got a letter from our friend in Norway, saying how much he had enjoyed our visit and our company. He also said that the boss from the factory had asked where Laszlo was, because he wanted to employ him and to give us a car and a home. We were quite amazed. We could have stayed in Norway and would have been all set up. The thought had never even occurred to us when we were there. In any case we couldn't go back into the Western countries for another three years. However this was the point when we started to seriously consider leaving Hungary for good. We were starting to get fed up with everything and after seeing what life was like in Western countries, we really began to believe that we could have a better life somewhere else. Our first priority was to sell the house. We didn't have any firm plans after that, but the idea of leaving the country was in the back of our minds. We didn't tell anybody, of course, not even our parents. We were unsure of where we would even go, but the idea stayed with us.

People were curious about why we wanted to sell the house and we would say that we just wanted to move somewhere else. This was true to a degree, we really did look around – we thought that maybe if we just moved somewhere that was far enough away from my parents then things might improve and we could have a different life with just the four of us. As it happened we didn't find anything that we wanted but we were genuinely open minded to either outcome.

One day some time after our trip my sister in law came over with the girls. She was crying and told us that my brother had gone. He had left Hungary and had gone to Austria so that he could try to immigrate to Australia. Once he had settled there he would send for the family. Laszlo and I looked at each other in alarm and both of us almost had a heart attack. That was our plan and nobody in the world knew about it, yet my brother had decided to do exactly the same thing. There were also other complications. In Hungary at that time if one member of your family left the country illegally and the government found out about it, then no other family member could get a passport. We didn't know what to say and decided not to admit that we wanted to do the same. Besides it appeared that our plan was now ruined and that we would never be able to get a visa or passport. Everybody was so surprised that my brother had done this, because absolutely nobody had any idea he was planning it. It was a real shock to the system.

Another complication was that if you left the country illegally then the government could reclaim your house. So my mother was running around trying to get papers backdated and had to forge my brother's signature so that their house wouldn't get taken away if the government found out. I'm not exactly sure how the system worked but there were some strange rules and my mother was trying to get around them.

A few days after my brother's shock departure we went to visit his wife and daughters. We couldn't believe our eyes when my brother answered the door! We were dumbfounded and asked him what was going on. Apparently he had made it to Austria and had gone to a special place and had started to set the wheels in motion for his plan. But he had missed his family too much and had returned after just a week. Because he had come back within the month, the government never found out about his intention to stay away illegally. Laszlo and I decided to talk to my brother and his wife and see if they wanted to try and leave the country together, (as he knew where to go, what to do & we could help each other out). This would give us time to sell our houses and to get the proper visas and other paperwork.

Chapter Three

We still had 18 months to wait before we could apply for blue passports again, so we just continued on as normal. Nobody suspected that we were planning to leave the country; they all thought that we just wanted to build a house somewhere else. In other people's eyes we were doing quite well – with a house, car and business – so why would we want to leave? We were lucky that nobody had reason to suspect us and we certainly didn't tell a soul what our plans were. Eventually my brother and his wife sold their house and so did we. My brother moved in with his in-laws in a granny flat which was a temporary measure while they supposedly looked around for somewhere else. We didn't have anywhere temporary to go so we moved into an apartment in Budapest. It was quite unusual to rent in Hungary in those days, but eventually we found a nice place that was furnished. This was lucky because we had sold our furniture with the house. We had also left our beautiful German Shepherd with the people who bought the house. They loved him and we thought that it would be for the best because we weren't sure where we would end up. It was sad for us, but we wanted him to have a good home.

We were happy enough in our nice apartment and life went on as normal for a while as we bided our time. Anita was at school and Csilla was at kindy. The Christmas after we moved, we had particularly harsh weather. One day we had almost one metre of snow and the temperature plunged to -35 C°. It was really windy and the snow just kept on falling. Anita went to school and I took Csilla to kindy. When I got back home the wind was so strong that I had to walk backwards so I could breathe. Laszlo came home shortly after me and said that he had a really bad feeling that Anita had gotten lost in the snow somewhere, even though school was close by. We got dressed in our coats and boots and tried to look for her. When we got to her school we found that she had arrived safely, but we decided to take her home with us. We also picked Csilla up on the way back. For a few days we just stayed home, hoping that the bad weather would pass. It felt awful to let the kids go out in such conditions. Because we were living in a townhouse we didn't have a garage, to keep the car in, so we had to find one nearby. At the time we had a red VW Golf. I really loved that car, it was comfortable and reliable and cute too! We finally found a garage a few streets away. It might seem quite strange to have to do that but in such bad weather conditions you had to. It was either that or you'd have to try dig your car out of the snow the next morning. We did have to do this a few times and it wasn't fun at all.

Our plan was to leave in the spring school holidays with my brother and his family. We would say we were going to Austria for a ski holiday, but would "forget" to come home again. These holidays would be around the end of March. In the meantime we had to apply for another visa. Our three-year wait for our passports was almost up, so we could get permission to leave again. We all put our papers in but we never really talked about it much because it was such a big secret and we didn't want to let anything slip. At first my brother's application was knocked back because his workplace wouldn't sign the forms for some reason. This was one of the rules and my brother was really upset because it was going to ruin our plans. Then Laszlo said that my brother could come and work for him, because he was also an electrician. So that's what we did and he got his papers signed by Laszlo. At that time my brother and his family were still living with his in-laws.

One day in January my brother didn't show up for work, so we went to see them. His mother in law opened the gate and we could see that she was crying. She said that she didn't know what had happened to them. They had disappeared during the night and had taken all their things. She didn't know where they were or what they were doing and was very upset. It was a big surprise for us because we did know where they were, but we couldn't say anything. We didn't know why they hadn't waited for us, but our hands were tied because we didn't have our passports or other necessary papers yet. Besides we didn't know exactly where we had to go. We knew that it was near Vienna but we didn't know the name of the place or any other important details. It was pretty scary to think that we would have to try and find these things out for ourselves. We weren't sure what to do. My parents found out that my brother had gone and we had to confess that we were planning to do the same when and if we could get our passports.

Things started to get a bit tense after my brother left because we were uncertain about what we would do. I wasn't working at the time, and we tried to carry on as normal. During this time Csilla got sick with tonsillitis. She was four, but was still really tiny and we were worried about her. The doctor said that her tonsils should come out. So we had to go to the hospital for blood and urine tests and unfortunately the nurses weren't very nice. First we tried for a urine sample, but Csilla didn't need to go to the toilet and couldn't understand why they were trying to make her. So we decided to do the blood test in the meantime, which wasn't pleasant. When it was over the nurse gave her some water and we tried for a urine sample again. Poor Csilla was very upset and started crying. She thought that if she didn't do a wee then they would stick the needle in her arm again. I tried to calm her down and explained that the blood tests were finished. Eventually she was OK and managed to produce the required urine sample.

At that time in Budapest it was relatively new that mothers could stay in hospital with their children when they were sick. So I packed my things as well and reassured Csilla that I would be with her. When we got to hospital she had to have another urine test and it showed up blood in her urine. Then without telling me anything they took Csilla away and came back a short time later carrying her clothes. They said that they were sorry but I couldn't stay because they had to find out what was wrong with her before they operated. This was such a traumatic experience for me. It was like a child had died and they had brought her clothes out. I didn't know where she was or how long she'd be there. She had thought that Mummy would be back with her and now I wasn't even allowed to say goodbye to her. She had no idea why I left her with these people that she didn't know. I was crying all the way home and when I arrived Laszlo called the doctor and we went back to the hospital. They said that they needed to clear her urine before the operation and wouldn't change their minds.

After five or six days nothing had changed. We had been there to see her as often as we were allowed, but it was just awful because she wasn't even allowed to have her own pyjamas. All the kids had the same yellow pyjamas and would be sitting in tiny little chairs waiting for their visitors. It was so heartbreaking because they were just like little zombies, they weren't smiling or anything. We tried to cheer her up when we visited but she was very distressed. She told us how they were woken up very early for a cold shower and were then put back to bed. After six days we couldn't stand it any more, so Laszlo called the doctor and said that if she didn't have the operation the next day then we would take her home because it was too much for us to bear. We also offered them some cash to speed things up. The operation was done the next day. Interestingly enough after the operation her urine was clear again — apparently it had been present because of the infection. So poor Csilla had suffered for nothing and I don't know how long it would have gone on if we hadn't done something. One day we went to put her back in her little bed and she tried to climb out again. We found out that they pushed them back into bed when they tried to get out. She was very distressed and we tried to calm her down. The whole experience was just awful and I would never wish it on anybody else.

Four days after the operation we could bring her home again, but the whole experience had affected her. She was still like a little zombie, she didn't want to play or have fun and would sit in her bed and just stare at the wall. It was almost like she was dreaming. We had another big snowfall and couldn't go anywhere, and Anita was really worried about her little sister. Thankfully after a few days back home Csilla started to get back to normal again.

Around this time we had a really big snowstorm that stopped everything, even buses and cars. It was a really horrific few days, but luckily we had a little shop nearby, so we could get basic supplies. Somehow my mum managed to make her way from her little village to where we lived with two 1kg loaves of bread, so we wouldn't starve. Once again it was nice of her – she had almost risked her life – but it wasn't necessary. It made us feel like we couldn't look after our family by ourselves and we knew that we could. Her actions made out that we couldn't feed our own kids. We thanked her but said that it really hadn't been necessary. She couldn't stay so she had to go back home again. We felt bad that she had to go out in such horrific weather conditions, but she had created the situation herself because of her need to always help us.

Time continued to go on and we still didn't hear anything from my brother. We asked his mother in law and she admitted that she knew where they were but it was such a big secret that she couldn't tell anybody. Eventually we got our own passports. Apparently they hadn't checked about my brother in time so we could still leave. But we were very uneasy and knew that we would have to leave soon because if they did find out about my brother then we would really be in trouble. One day not long before we planned to leave I was home with Csilla when the doorbell rang. We had a security system on our building so visitors had to ring first. We rarely had visitors though, because very few people knew where we were. I looked outside to see who was there and almost had a heart attack when I saw two policemen standing there. I was really scared when I saw them and felt sure that it must be about my brother. I didn't want to let them in but I had to and I was certain that our plans to leave would now be foiled. It was such a relief when I spoke to them to find out that they were actually looking for the previous tenants of the apartment. Apparently they had been involved in car thefts. Funnily enough I had come across some car registration plates in one of the cupboards when we had moved in, which I gave to the policemen. When I told Laszlo we were both so relieved that we hadn't been found out, but it did reinforce in our minds that we had to do something very soon.

Because we had sold our house we did have money in the bank. However the Hungarian currency (Forint) wasn't easily convertible throughout other European countries and it didn't have a very high exchange value. So there wasn't much point in taking a large amount of money with us. Instead we decided to buy gold, because that was something that held its value all over the world. We had about 1.5 million Forint - which sounds like a lot - but it wasn't really. We spent about 500,000. - on jewellery – necklaces, bracelets and a beautiful white gold watch with little diamonds around the face. We were still concerned, however, about how we could take it with us without the border guards finding it, so we worked out a plan. Laszlo parked the car close to the house a few days before we left and found a hollow space in the back section of the car that had a plastic cover. We packed all our cash and jewellery into little plastic bags and pushed them into this hollow space. We had bought some foam filler that would cover all the hollow areas which held the money and jewellery in position. We then put the cover back on and were reasonably sure that nobody would notice what we had done. The scary thing was that we had to leave the car in the street for a few days before we left. The rent of the garage had run out. We could only hope that it wouldn't be stolen, because car theft was quite common in Budapest at that time. If that had happened we would have really been in a terrible predicament.

Time was really becoming crucial and we knew that we would be leaving any day. Laszlo's parents' 40th wedding anniversary was coming up on the 29th of March so we brought beautiful gold rings for both of them. We then gave them the little package and told them not to open it until their anniversary. We also had a godchild whose family was in quite a bad situation. They needed about 60,000. -Forint to get a better place and start a new life. So we opened a chequebook account in our goddaughter's name and left 60,000. - Forint in the bank. We told Laszlo's mum that the money was for our goddaughter's family. They didn't know why we were doing it, but they thought that it was very nice of us.

On the 28th of March we decided to go. During the day I packed all our clothes and tried to think of what we would need. I decided on mainly summer clothes as we were planning on going to Australia, even though it was still only early spring in Europe and quite cold. We couldn't take everything so we had to make some compromises. It also might have been a problem if the border guards asked us why we were taking summer clothes for a skiing holiday. I packed about five suitcases in total and when night came we snuck down and put them in the car. This was hard to do because our front door squeaked and it would have seemed suspicious to our neighbours that we were going to and from the car several times so late at night. Slowly but surely we packed the car. We put the back seat down so the kids could sleep and packed the space between the front and back seats with suitcases. Then we put pillows and quilts in that the girls could sleep on. We had our own TV, fridge and washing machine that we had to leave behind as well as excess clothes and some other personal stuff that we just couldn't take. The main thing that we took with us was our clothes. It was strange to look around our little apartment and know that we were leaving forever but we just said, "let's go". Eventually we got into the car and drove off late that night. Our amazing and somewhat dangerous journey was about to begin. We had even bought skiis and strapped it to the roof to authenticate the story that we were going skiing in Austria.

We lived about 150km from the border so we had a bit of a drive ahead of us. We were both incredibly nervous because we knew that this time we weren't planning to come back. It felt like we looked really suspicious, almost as if our plans were written across our foreheads and that everybody would guess what we were doing. It really is hard to explain just how nerve-wracking our escape from Hungary was.

We reached the border in about two or three hours, although just before we got there I realised that I had left my low blood pressure medication behind. We couldn't go back though so I just had to go without it. Even though it was so late at night, there was still a queue that we had to wait in before we crossed the border. This made us even more nervous. Eventually the soldiers checked us through. They were very kind young soldiers and asked us where we were going. We told them we were going to Austria on a ski holiday. They asked Laszlo and I to get out so they could check our height and hair/eye colour, but they didn't wake up the girls. They then asked us to open up the back of the car. That was when my leg started to shake and for a while I wasn't sure if it would hold me up anymore. Laszlo opened the back door and the guards went through everything. They lifted things up and poked under the pillows with a torch. They also looked under the car and went very close to the space where we had hidden the money and jewellery. It was an extremely scary and stressful situation but we had no control over what happened and eventually it was over. To our overwhelming relief they couldn't find anything amiss, so they closed the door, stamped our passports and let us through. The road away from the border zigzagged back and forth. You had to go left, then right and so on. It was obviously constructed that way so if somebody tried to escape and drive away they would be shot in the process, because of the delay in leaving. We just kept driving – neither of us said a word and we didn't even dare look at each other. We then had to go through the Austrian border, but we only had to show our passports there so it wasn't stressful at all.

Chapter Four

We continued driving through the night. It was raining lightly so we had to use the windscreen wipers. One of them was a bit squeaky which really added to the tension that we were already feeling. We had just arrived in a little city outside of Vienna when the police waved us over. Once again our stress levels went up and we panicked. But luckily it was just a general check of the car to make sure that everything was working properly and also that we had the correct car registration papers. Everything was fine and the police just waved us on and wished us a nice holiday. We could breathe easy again!

We arrived in Vienna at about five or six o'clock in the morning. We didn't have a clue where we had to go or what we had to do so we just kept driving for a while, looking for a place that we could stop at and have a sleep and relax a bit. We stopped a few times but no-one had any spare rooms. We had no idea where we were but finally we found a tiny little town on the outskirts of Vienna. It had beautiful houses, buildings and churches and was very quaint. There was a tiny motel, so we parked our car outside a little church and enquired about rooms. They actually only had two rooms in the motel but one of them was free - to our great relief. They let us in with no problems and we bought our suitcases inside as well. That was when we discovered that the suitcases we had put between the front and back seats had somehow gotten wet from the rain. All the kids' clothes and some of ours were wet and smelly and so was the car.

Fortunately the room had a radiator heater, so we spread out as many of the clothes as we could to dry before we went to sleep. We woke up a few hours later and went down to have our breakfast in the tiny, old restaurant in the motel. There were a few locals around who were really friendly. They knew we couldn't speak German and communicated with us the best that they could. They had lots of rolls, meat and fruit and we ate as much as we could because we were all hungry. It was a lovely meal.

After breakfast we went back to our room to make some plans. First of all we drove around this little town a bit to see if we could work our where we were. We tried very hard to remember the name of the place that my brother had mentioned. We thought it was 'lager' something but nobody seemed to know. We then remembered the name of the place was Starkirhen, but whenever we asked people they would say a different place that sounded similar. We also went around the banks and checked if we could change some of our

Hungarian currency. We only tried to change small amounts to begin with and they did it. We had hoped that we could change larger amounts if we needed to in the future. It was really nice spring weather so we were only wearing lighter clothes and shoes. Suddenly out of nowhere it began to snow. We ran into a shop to take shelter and bought the girls some gumboots to keep their feet dry. We also had wet shoes now, to go along with out wet clothes. At the end of the day we still didn't know where we had to go or what we had to do.

The next day we decided that we would go to the police station to see if they could help us. We were a bit unsure about this move because we didn't know if they would report us to the Hungarian police. But it was a risk we had to take; otherwise we would be stuck in this place and might never find out where we had to go. So we went into the nearest police station and it soon became obvious that our language barrier was a problem. We tried to use sign language and hand signals to explain that we were looking for Starkirhen. But they had no idea what we were talking about. This was quite a surprise for us because we assumed that the police would know about this place. My brother had said that it was a huge building and well known, so we couldn't understand why nobody seemed to know what we were talking about, least of all the police. It was very frustrating, as apparently large numbers of people went there from many different Eastern European countries. We made no progress with the police and eventually left, feeling a bit worried. Once again we were thinking – 'now what?'

We walked outside the police station feeling quite despondent and continued to walk around for a while. As we walked we came across a place that was a shelter of some sort, like the Salvation Army or something similar. We decided to go in and were greeted by a nice young guy, but once again language was a problem. We tried to explain that we were looking for Starkirhen but he didn't understand at all. He asked where we were from, so we told him but apparently he thought we were begging for food. I guess seeing that we had two little kids with us and because we looked sad and lost, it was an easy mistake to make. In any case we were a bit surprised when he bought us some food. We tried to say that we were grateful, but we weren't looking for food – we were looking for this place called Starkirhen. He just nodded and obviously didn't understand what we were saying.

When he worked out that we were Hungarian, he remembered that there was a Hungarian woman working close by in one of the other offices. He then took us to see her and we were finally able to explain properly what we were looking for. We told this woman our story, explaining that we had our passports and that we didn't want to go back home but that we wanted to apply for residency in Austria and then hopefully immigrate somewhere else. She didn't know exactly what to do but asked if we had a car and our stuff. My brother had said that you weren't supposed to admit that you had a car, because it looked better if you seemed to be really poor. So we said that we didn't have a car but we did have our things in a motel. After translation, the young guy worked out where we wanted to go and what we wanted to do and said that he could take us. He said that we could go back and get our stuff and then he would give us a lift to this place and take us inside.

We rushed back to the motel and quickly packed our things. Some of it was dry and some was still wet, but we just had to pack it like it was. It was worrying to have to leave the car behind but we couldn't do anything about it. We didn't know where we were going or what lay ahead of us, but now that things were in motion we couldn't look back. We drove through the city and eventually came to a very bad looking area; it was scary just to drive there. We then ended up in front of a huge gate. When we went through this gate we saw soldiers with guns over their shoulders. They spoke to the guy and asked him what was going on and he explained our circumstances. They then asked for our passports and we handed them over, but they didn't give them back. We were then directed to drive through the gate. It was a huge old building that was made of brick and was very dirty looking. All around it were smaller buildings of the same style. Some parts were like two and three level houses and people obviously lived there as some of them were doing washing and hanging it outside. We were still driving at this stage and when we saw these people they seemed quite scary looking, like they were really poor and desperate. It was all quite overwhelming because at that point we didn't know where we were or what was happening to us. It was the 1st of April 1987, which was Anita's ninth birthday.

Eventually we had to get out of the car and we also had to take our luggage out too. Our driver said "good luck" and then he left. There were people standing around as well as lots of soldiers with guns. They asked us to go into the big building and as we went across we could see some cars parked in front of the buildings. There were high fences around the area that we were in, so we knew that we couldn't leave. At that time we were quite apprehensive about what was going to happen to us. We had to go up the stairs and we noticed that all the windows had bars on them. There were more soldiers with guns in each area we passed through, and as we went through each gate it would be closed behind us. Eventually we ended up in a little office where they tried to ask us some questions. But they were speaking German and we couldn't understand them. Finally we started to communicate a little. The girls were both really nervous. Anita was only nine and Csilla just four and a half and they had no idea what was going on. We were also really apprehensive as we had no idea what we had done or what would be the outcome of this situation.

The soldiers asked us to stand next to the wall so they could take our measurements. They then took photos – both front and profile – as well as taking our fingerprints. We had never done that before, but they were quite helpful with the whole procedure. We had no idea why we were being fingerprinted; we certainly weren't criminals. But we found out later that they did this to everybody, as they had to send the fingerprints to Interpol to be checked. Anybody with a criminal background was sent back to their own country. After this we were taken to another room where we tried to wash the fingerprint ink off our hands. It was very difficult to do. We were then taken into another room where we were given blankets and aluminium plates, cups and cutlery. They then showed us to our room. It was a reasonably small room with two sets of bunk beds near the windows and another set on the right hand side of the door. On the left of the door was a table with a few chairs and that was about it. There was already another couple there, so we introduced ourselves. They were using the bunks near the door so we took the others. The kids had the top and we had the bottom. I honestly can't remember if the other couple there were Hungarian or not. We just sat down and looked at each other – we were just numb and overwhelmed with all that had happened to us. We had no idea what would happen next, but we had made it this far and that was definitely a start.

We found out that the place we had come to wasn't called Starkirhen; it was actually called Traiskirchen. That was why nobody had understood us. We had a conversation with the other couple and discovered that we were very lucky to have gotten the room that we did, because the other rooms were really big and had about 40 or 50 people in each. Men, women and children were all together in these other rooms. We were also quite lucky to have a shower on our floor. Every morning one of the family members (usually the husband) went downstairs to the ground floor to collect some breakfast in a brown paper bag. Usually it was a roll and a jug of cocoa or milky coffee that the girls could drink as well. We didn't have much of an appetite as we were quite stressed, but we had to make ourselves eat something.

We ventured out into the corridor on our level during the day and started to meet other people and found out what was going on. That was how we gained information about the Interpol checks. There were lots of people in this place – families with kids, couples and singles as well. They were from all different Eastern European countries such as Romania, Poland, Czechoslovakia, Yugoslavia and Albania. But we were all hoping for the best. We weren't allowed to leave level three, except for meals when Laszlo would go down to get the food in the morning. We found out that we had to be locked up for five days and on one of those days we would have to have a medical check up. Apparently if your Interpol checks were cleared then you were given your check up. After that they would find you a place to live until your immigration was arranged. We also had to register where we wanted to go. We had the chance to either apply for Canada, America or Australia. We didn't really want Canada because we knew it would be very cold there. We were hoping for somewhere with a warmer climate. Another one of my uncles lived in America and we had previously enquired about how many judo clubs were there (for Laszlo) and also about my chances of finding work. He replied that he didn't know anybody who did karate and that he couldn't really help us. He also said that America had changed and that we would be better off going somewhere else. So we had already made up our minds to apply for Australia only and just hoped for the best. We didn't know what would happen if we missed out but decided to just wait and see. We met many different people who were all very helpful and were in the same boat as us. We remember one Hungarian family particularly well. They were staying in the large room that housed about 40 or 50 people. They had a young son who was tiny like Csilla and who was a bit younger than her. He was an adorable little boy who really captivated us. Although this was a confusing place for a child to be, he seemed quite comfortable and acted like he was very at home. His parents were really nice as well. They were from Budapest. One of the guards on the third level used to allow the men to set up some tables to play cards. We didn't realise, however, that this was actually not allowed as they considered it to be a form of gambling. This really wasn't an issue, it was just something that the men were doing to pass the time, not to try and make money. On one occasion another one of the guards saw them playing and went right off his head. He yelled and shouted at the guys and accused them of gambling as well as other things. It almost got to the point where he was going to give back our passports and papers and make us leave. Fortunately that didn't happen, as we were all determined to stay. We all had to bite our tongues and not answer this guard back, as we didn't want to get in any more trouble. When we were still locked on the third level, some of the other guys who had left and were now free to go outside went out and bought some cigarettes and other things like Coca Cola. Then some of the people on the third level lowered down a basket, their coke and cigarettes were placed in it and they pulled it back up again. We didn't smoke so it didn't affect us, but there were quite a few people who benefited from it. There were also quite a few people of gypsy nationality on our level and we found them a bit scary. They were quite nasty looking and used to look at people when they were in the shower. I really had to protect the kids from them, because we didn't know what they might do. We thought they would steal from us or try to hurt the children.

On about the third day that we were there the police came in and took away an Albanian man, who had apparently killed a few people. This was an interesting experience but we weren't worried about our safety while we were in there as there were so many soldiers around and there were lots of police as well. When we went down for lunch and dinner we would have to get in a queue – there would be police at the beginning, in the middle and at the end of the queue. It was like being in jail. Although I had never actually been into a jail, it was what I imagined that it must be like. Despite this we were very grateful to be getting food (as simple as it was). Once when we were sitting down eating, I wanted to get the salt or something and went to stand up so I could reach it. I then discovered that the chairs were all nailed to a piece of wood, so if one person wanted to move then everybody had to move. Things like that were quite scary and robbed you of your dignity. We weren't criminals or bad people but we were treated in that way because the soldiers and police didn't know if we were or not. That was their job and they couldn't afford to take chances. But it did make you feel like less of a person all the same. After we ate our meals, we had to wash our own dishes, but there wasn't any hot water. This was a bit of a worry, because we had to use the same utensils for five days. I did my best to keep everything as clean as possible and I just hoped that we wouldn't get sick.

At the same time that we had arrived in Traiskirchen, my mother had arrived at our apartment in Budapest with a birthday cake for Anita. When she rang the bell nobody answered and she was worried. She rang the bell of our next-door neighbours. They were an old couple and we had given them an emergency key. They let Mum in and she could see that there were things missing. She knew that we were planning to leave, but she didn't know when. It was a horrific experience for her to find out in that way. We regretted this, but it was the only way that we could arrange our departure. Soon afterwards my parents had to pack up our remaining things, and I know that it must have been a heartbreaking experience for them.

Eventually we were asked to go down to have our medical checks with some other people. We were escorted down by the soldiers and there were police present during the tests as well, so it wasn't very pleasant but it had to be done. We had to give a urine sample, chest x-ray but surprisingly no blood tests. AIDS was around then so it seemed unusual that they weren't checking for that. Then we had to wait for a while before doing a sight test. They then asked us how we felt to which we replied that we were nervous, but felt OK. A few hours later the results came back. We were cleared through Interpol and were also deemed to be medically healthy. On the fifth day we were allowed to leave the locked area. We went down and got all our papers, but not our passports. We had more photos taken and were given an Austrian ID card called a Fluchtlingslager. It was like a driver's licence that showed we were temporary residents of Austria. We went down to the lower section and were told that we had to stay there one more night before they gave us an address that we could go to.

When we were free to go the next morning, Laszlo went back to get the car. Amazingly it was still there and apparently nobody had touched it. Even the skiis were still attached to the roof. Laszlo drove the car back and parked it nearby, removing all the gold and cash first.

We were very nervous about parking on the
street as it was such a bad area, but we couldn't
take it inside because we had said that we
didn't have a car. We found out later that it
didn't matter if you had a car or not. But at the
time we were going on what my brother had
told us. We had asked around to see if
anybody had heard of my brother, but nobody
had. We still didn't know where they were, but
we knew that they definitely weren't at
Traiskirchen.

We were a bit scared when we slept in the
'free' area because the night before somebody
had been killed. We were all sleeping in the
same bed and had put a blanket around the top
bunk to make a curtain so that nobody could
see in. We had our entire luggage in there with
the gold as well as the cash and us. I even left
my boots on so that nobody could steal them.
It was a bad night for us, we hardly slept at all
and we were really worried about the car being
outside on the road.

Before we left we went into the office to find
out where we had to go. There were another
two Hungarian couples there, one of whom had
a young son. There were three cars between us
and we found out that we were going to the
same place. They knew we had a car so they
waited for us while we went outside and
packed up. Once again we had been lucky and
the car was still there. We looked at a map so
we could work out where we had to go. We
were being sent to a little town called
Almunstern, but we couldn't find it on the map.
We asked the soldiers and they explained that it
was about 250 or 300 km away. We went into
a little shop and got some food and then set off
on our journey. We drove in a convoy with the
two other cars and took turns at being the first
car. We stopped a few times for snacks and a
cup of coffee and at one of the places we asked
where Almunstern was. They didn't know but
said that it definitely wasn't the way we were
heading. They advised us to go back to the
main road and head towards Linz, as they

thought that maybe somebody there could help us, forcing us to backtrack a bit.

We went through a little town called Gmunden; it had a beautiful lake and was a really nice little town. We asked directions and to our relief we found that Almunstern was only a few kilometres away. Finally we arrived at our temporary home which was to be for an unknown amount of time. Close to the huge building that accommodated us, was a beautiful lake. There was also a mountain in the distance, which still had snow on the top. The general surroundings were breathtaking; there were lots of trees and greenery. The weather was also great on the day we arrived. We were amazed and couldn't believe that we were staying there. The motel itself was a long, two-storey building, which had balconies that faced the road. There was also a little pub/restaurant in the middle and a tiny creek running under the building.

Once we got our bearings we went to look for a parking space and as we drove into the parking lot I was absolutely stunned to see my sister in law and one of her daughters. The four of us froze and so did they. It had been such a huge secret where they were and now out of the 250 or 300 places that we could have been sent, we had ended up in the same building! It was an incredible coincidence and it seemed that fate must have surely had a hand in us both being there. All I could say to Laszlo was, "my brother is here!" We didn't really know what to do about it though, we didn't say anything much whilst we parked the car as we didn't know how much we were allowed to reveal. We then went to the little restaurant and got our room assigned to us (room 204). It was quite a small room on the first level, with a double bed and some bunks for the girls. It also had a tiny bathroom and a balcony. We had to do our washing up and wash our clothes in the little sink, but at least we had somewhere nice to stay. We were facing the road and had a beautiful view. Although it was small it was comfortable and we were very happy to have such nice accommodation.

Chapter Five

I had said to Laszlo that if I ever saw my brother again, I would really like to punch him for abandoning us like that. When we settled down in our room, I decided that I would go and find him and confront him. I went and asked around in the little coffee shop to find out where he and his family were. They told me which room he was in and showed me the way to go. They were living on the other side of the building. I had to go down a narrow, dark corridor but I finally found the room. When I got there my heart was in my mouth. I was really nervous but I knew that I had to do it. I knocked on the door and they asked who it was. Then I went inside. My brother and his wife were sitting on the bed and they looked at me timidly like they were little grey mice. They were obviously more worried than me about what was going to happen between us. I simply looked at them - at that point I really didn't know what I felt. I had mixed emotions. Then I asked them why they had done it. Why did they leave us there? My brother looked at me and said that they were really scared. I just stood there for a while and looked at them. I didn't know what to say. They didn't say anything else to me, so I just turned around, closed the door and left. I was quite numb and slowly went back to our room and told Laszlo what happened. He said not to worry about it. The point was that we had made it there and we could get on with our new lives. We didn't speak to my brother for a while and this was quite uncomfortable, considering that we were in the same building.

We were given some crockery and cutlery and at each mealtime we had to go down to the kitchen area and queue to get our food. We could then bring it back up to our room and eat it there. The food tasted very good. Dinner was always cooked and sometimes lunch was cooked too. Some of the people who had been there for a while were allowed to work and some of the women worked in the kitchen. They didn't get paid much and others were just volunteers. A lot of the men would go out to the front each morning and ask people in the passing cars if they needed workers for the forestry or building sites. If there was something available they would take men from there and give them some work to do. They didn't pay them very much though. Laszlo found this situation quite embarrassing. He said that he never wanted to do that, we had a little bit of money saved and could survive OK, so he never went down and stood out the front. We met quite a few people during our stay there and heard many different stories about how long we might be there. Some people had been there for 2 ½ years and some for three. It seemed that there were many different outcomes. We were quite concerned when we heard this, because we really didn't want to have to stay there for that long. It seemed that a lot of people were quite pessimistic about the whole situation; we never got to hear good stories about people who had been granted the country of their choice. Their attitude seemed to be that if they had been there for three years, then we would have to wait our turn and stay there for that long as well. We were quite concerned, as we still didn't really know how the system worked. When they found out that Anita was from my first husband, they were even more negative. They said that there was no way I would be allowed to leave Austria, that no country would accept me because my first husband would have to sign a paper allowing her to leave. I was quite worried when I heard this because he had been quite nasty the last time when we were going on our holiday, and this time he didn't even know that we had left the country permanently. If this was true and he wouldn't sign the papers, then we would be stuck there and unable to even go back to Hungary without facing imprisonment. Anita was very upset by all this. She was crying about it and said that if she wasn't allowed to go then she didn't want to have to stay in Austria or go back to her Dad. I reassured her that if her father wouldn't allow her to leave then we would go back and face the music. But we would never go anywhere without her. The four of us were a family and it was either all or none of us.

Some time passed by and we still weren't speaking to my brother. We found out that he was working in the building, as he was quite friendly with the owner. He was doing maintenance and other similar type of work. Most of the men left in the morning to do some kind of work and some of them said to Laszlo that he would never get a job by just waiting around. Nobody would come and knock on the door to offer him a job. They gave all kinds of advice and Laszlo just said, "OK". One day we were in our room watching TV when there was literally a knock on the door. It was somebody from the cottage area. There was a nice young couple looking for help and nobody else was home except for Laszlo. It was quite ironic really, that somebody did come along and knock on the door and offer Laszlo a job. He went and worked for this really nice young German couple. Laszlo knew a little bit of German and he tried to talk to them as best he could. They seemed to understand our situation. The Austrian people tended to be a bit mean to us and tried to make us feel humiliated sometimes. I guess we could understand their attitude as they were taxpayers and their money was keeping us there, feeding us and housing us. However the system had been in place for a long time and had obviously been set up to help those who had managed to leave the Eastern bloc countries. We had found that many German people had the attitude that they were better than others; that everybody else was below them. But this couple weren't like that at all. They were just lovely. They invited us to have a look at their place. Anita had the opportunity to go to the primary school. The lessons were all in German, of course, but kids pick up languages very fast and we soon had some more knowledge of the language.

I didn't like the situation with my brother. It was uncomfortable not to be speaking to them and I started to think that we had to consider the future. What was done was done and I didn't want to hold a grudge any more. The main thing was that we were all here and we were all healthy. We gradually started to talk again. We didn't talk about the past, just about normal everyday things. We sometimes went shopping together, although we couldn't really buy much. We knew that if we were accepted somewhere then we would have to fly out and wouldn't be able to take much with us. There was a really nice shopping centre nearby, which was nice to have a look around or have a coffee. We also found out that the people in the area would often put out really good things when they had organised 'clean up' days. They would put good electrical appliances that still worked, out to be collected. Usually they had just bought a new one and didn't want the old one anymore. We got a little tiny fridge this way and later on we got a TV. The motel had cable TV, although our room wasn't connected. But somehow Laszlo got up through a window late one night and managed to connect us, even though we weren't supposed to have it. This gave us a bigger choice of TV shows to watch. We had Sky channel, which only had one Australian show – A Country Practice. We were very keen to watch it because we wanted to find out all we could about Australia – what were the people like, what did they do, what did they wear? At that time we knew absolutely nothing about Australia. In Europe we rarely heard anything about other countries and we had never seen any Australian TV shows. People in general didn't really know much about Australia. To them it was just 'Down Under'. From what other people said we had the idea that there was nothing there, just lots of sheep, kangaroos jumping down the streets, rusty windmills, old cars and lots of tumbleweed blowing around! We were quite happy to see A Country Practice and notice that the people there dressed like anybody else in the world and did the same sorts of things. We tried our best to catch onto the language by following the scenes and piecing together what they were talking about. But it was quite difficult to do!

Laszlo was still working for this nice couple and one day he came home early and I noticed that he was hopping up the stairs. When I asked him what had happened he explained that he had been nailing up on the roof and had somehow put his ankle out. Despite this he had managed to drive home. We had to take him straight to the hospital, even though we had no idea who would pay for it. We had no knowledge of what we needed to do in case of injury or illness. Somebody drove us to the hospital quite late at night and they had to put his ankle back in position and then put plaster on it. This plaster had to stay on for three weeks, which was a bit of a problem because he had to go back to work and finish off the job that he was working on. But there was nothing we could do about it. I also had to drive the car, which was very scary for me. At that time I had hardly any driving experience and our car was also a manual, which made it even more difficult, but I didn't have any other choice. Each morning I had to get up and take Anita and a few other kids to school and also pick them up in the afternoon. It was quite common there that people who didn't have cars would pay those who did to take them places they wanted to go. It was basically like a cab service and many people did it.

One day while Laszlo was recovering there was a knock on the door and it was the nice young couple that he had been working for. They had a box of chocolates for me and a nice bottle of home made red wine for Laszlo. They said not to worry about him taking time off because they weren't going to look for somebody else. They were very happy with Laszlo's work and would wait until he was fit again. We were so happy to hear this and it was nice to know that they valued Laszlo's work so much. They actually stopped building their extension and waited until Laszlo was ready before they began again.

On one occasion when Laszlo had recovered and had a day off, he drove some people to Vienna (300km away) and we charged them some money for the ride. We didn't know how much we were supposed to ask for so we just had to guess. After they came back that night, they must have told somebody how much Laszlo charged and my brother found out. He came rushing around to our room and just burst in without knocking. He said to Laszlo to never, ever do a trip like that again for such a low price. He said that he would ruin everybody else's business in the building and that he couldn't just come in and do it. Who did he think he was? It was the privilege of the people who had been there longer and he was just breaking all the rules. We were really stunned at the way my brother spoke to us. He could have simply come over and explained nicely what the system was, without resorting to threats and being so nasty about it.

We soon found out that where we were staying was not a huge secret (which is what my brother and his wife had told his mother-in-law when they first left). Both our parents were allowed to come and visit us when we were staying in Almunstern. My mother came over to see us first. It was pretty easy for her to travel to Austria because she could catch the train, as there was a station close by. She bought a beautiful fresh cake with her for Anita's birthday. Even though a few weeks had passed, she still wanted to give her a cake. At the border the guards asked what was going on and she explained that her granddaughter had just had her birthday and she wanted to surprise her with a cake. They just smiled and let her through; there wasn't any problem at all. She had a really good time on her visit. We took her all around the place, including a visit to the zoo and we also climbed some of the mountains. It really was a beautiful area that we were staying in. There was a pretty little lake close by, where you could go and have a swim, but the water was ice cold so we just went there to sunbake and have fun with the kids. We had a really nice time with Mum, even though we were in such an unusual situation. After about a week she had to go home and was very upset. At that time we didn't know where we would end up or if and when we would see each other again, but at least we could say a proper goodbye this time. We were all in tears when she left but we knew that as long as we were healthy that anything was possible. My mother saw my brother as well, but she didn't forget what he had done to us. I never forget things either but I try to forgive people whenever I can, but my Mum is a bit harder. She grew up in a different time and found it hard to forgive. One day while Mum was visiting she was sitting in our room with us when my brother and his wife burst into the room again without knocking. They then started saying that my parents never gave him anything and that I had been the only one they cared about. He accused Mum of not

loving him or his wife and many other hurtful
things. Once again we were just stunned. We
had no idea where any of this had come from
and none of it was true anyway. Even if it had
been true, we were in a situation where we
didn't know when we might see our parents
again, so it wasn't the time to be so nasty. Why
it was necessary to do this I really don't know.
I actually felt sorry for them, because for them
to do this they must have had no love in their
hearts at all. It was really strange and came
right out of the blue. Then they just got up and
left, without saying anything at all. I think that
they had said so many terrible things they had
started to believe that they were true. After
they left my Mum was really upset and said
that she had done everything the same for both
of us and I said that I knew that, because I had
been there too. We always got given the same
treats; sometimes he got more than me because
he would steal mine, as I was a slow eater.
Sometimes I would just give it to him because I
had a big heart.

My Dad also came to visit us a little while later and we had a wonderful time with him too. Not long after that Laszlo's mother and one of his brothers came to see us, they drove across in their little car. We could even get a separate room just for them. Laszlo's other brother also came to see us. It was good that everybody who wanted to see us got the chance and could say a proper goodbye. Laszlo's Dad couldn't come as he was quite old and his health wasn't good.

While we were waiting there, we were always on the lookout for a business sized white envelope. It was what everybody there was anxious to get because it meant that you had been invited for an interview in Vienna, to assess whether you were suitable to immigrate to the country of your choice. People from the country that you wanted to go to would interview the whole family and decide whether you could go or not. We would get our mail when we went to lunch. Each time we would be anxious to see if the white envelope was

there. Finally one day our white envelope
arrived. I was so nervous and shaky when I
opened it up. The letter inside said that we
were invited back to Traiskirchen for our
Australian interview. Believe it or not my
brother and his family got an interview the day
before us. They came back that night and were
really happy because they were accepted. They
had another health check as well. If everything
was OK with your second health check then
you left about eight weeks later. This was
because all the paperwork and other checks had
to be processed first. If everything was OK
with that, then they would find you seats on a
plane and you were allowed to leave.
Before we had our interview I had written to
my best friend Maria in Budapest and had
asked her to send me a nice fashionable dress
to wear. I wanted to look good for the
interview and we didn't have many clothes
with us at that time. She sent me back a really
nice dress. It was white with black dots on it
and it suited me really well. I was so happy
with it and the girls also looked lovely in their

clean dresses. Laszlo was wearing a suit and tie, so we all looked very presentable. We were extremely nervous as I still didn't have any papers from my ex-husband about Anita. But we were also hopeful because my brother had been successful.

We left in the morning and it was very strange to go back to Traiskirchen after all those weeks. It reminded us of our time up on the third floor and we knew we never wanted to go back there. We were so nervous while we were waiting but eventually went inside. There was an Australian interviewer and we also had an interpreter. First of all he asked us personal details and then checked on our education levels and what other qualifications we had. It was just like the points identification system in the bank. Some things got higher points than others. Education gave us more points. They asked us why we wanted to go to Australia and we replied that we had heard that Australia was a really beautiful country and that the people were really nice and friendly and we just wanted to live in a place like that. The truth was that we didn't know anything about the people in Australia, but we had to say something that sounded good. Then we got to the subject of Anita. The man asked me if my ex-husband would let her go. I was really white and shaking but I just said, "Yes, it is possible". After that they didn't ask anything else about it. Then they were just sitting there looking through the papers again. We were so nervous and were sweating while we waited, as it was also a really hot day. The kids just sat there, they didn't really know what was going on. They also asked if we had applied for any other countries. We told them that it was our first choice, we really wanted to go to Australia. Finally, after waiting for what seemed like a very long time while they looked through the papers again, they told us that we were accepted! We didn't even have to pay anything, as the government had accepted us. We were so incredibly relieved that I find it almost impossible to describe. We got given our papers and had to go and have our other medical check and by that time we were walking on the clouds and were incredibly happy. It was an amazing feeling and we didn't care about anything anymore. We didn't stop smiling all the way back to the hotel. We told everybody we knew that we had been accepted and had had our medical checks. My sister in law made the comment that we must have lied to have been accepted. I looked at her in surprise and said that they hadn't asked anything that I had to lie about and why would I lie in the first place. They had just asked common questions like my date of birth and educational standard. This conversation was another interesting experience with them. We found out later that a lot of people did lie when they went to the Australian interview. Many of them had applied for America or Canada as well and weren't accepted there so they tried for Australia. However when they were asked if they had applied somewhere else they said no. The people at the different embassies knew one another and they could easily check this information. Therefore it didn't look good for them when they weren't truthful about where they had applied for residency. This was why many of them were delayed for so long in migrating somewhere. No country wanted to accept them if they were prepared to lie in their first sentence.

One couple had actually stayed in the motel for about three or four years, but they had quite a sad reason. When they arrived they had a two year old son, who had been killed not long afterwards when he ran across the road. Since he was buried in Austria they were allowed to stay there with him.

We were so happy and all our friends there congratulated us. After we were accepted we asked why some people had to wait for years and others didn't. It turned out that they all had some kind of problem with their application. They were either divorced or separated or had some kind of illness. They all had problems that had to be solved before they could emigrate somewhere else. Because we didn't have any such problems, there was no need for us to wait such a long time. At this stage we were talking to my brother but we weren't really friendly. We had some mutual friends so it was very difficult not to talk and there wasn't any point holding a grudge anyway. While we were waiting to leave Laszlo went back to work and also found a Judo club where he could keep fit. We would sometimes get phone calls from people back home. The phone was downstairs and somebody would call out to us when we had a call. There was always someone there to answer the phone and they would come and get you. It was really nice to talk to people back home. My friend Maria said to us that we were so brave; she didn't think she could do what we had done. She was pregnant at the time and I really missed her. I would have loved to see her and had a good chat in person rather than on the phone, but we had chosen to do this and we knew there were some hard things to deal with.

We had also managed to find a beautiful book about Australia in a little bookshop in Gmunden. It was full of the most gorgeous photos and we were quite spellbound when we looked at them. Everything just looked incredible and we realised that there was definitely more than dried tumbleweed and rusty water tanks in this country. We believed that we had made a wonderful choice in selecting this as the country to emigrate to.

About eight weeks after our interview we were sitting in our room watching TV when someone came running up and knocked on the door. Laszlo happened to be home for lunch when this person ran in and said, "You guys are flying, you guys are flying!" We just looked at him and said to not joke about it, as it wasn't funny to trick us like that. The eight weeks were hardly up and nobody ever got to leave so fast. But the guy insisted that it was us, because nobody else there had that name - he said that there were four of us up on the board downstairs. It turned out that another Hungarian couple's name were on the same board and had picked up the papers. When we ran downstairs like idiots we couldn't see our names on the board. We then thought that it really was a joke and that it wasn't very funny. But the guy insisted that he had seen the paper with our names on it and we then found out that this other couple were so excited that they had taken the paper down and were running around with it, showing it to all their friends. We just couldn't believe that it was actually happening; the whole thing was very surreal. After we had settled down a bit we phoned my parents and told them that we were leaving in September. However when my brother found out about our exciting news, he and his family weren't happy at all. The corridor downstairs was about 90cm wide and my 16 year old niece spat on us as we walked past, when they heard that we were leaving earlier than them. We still had a few more weeks to wait before we left, but I couldn't believe how pathetic they were to do such a thing. Nobody can predict these things, we had absolutely no control over it but they were treating us like it was our fault. The Australian government had decided and it was something that was totally out of our hands. It was hell after that. I could not understand their attitude.

After we found out that we were leaving, we had to sell our car. We were actually very lucky because one of our friend's friend lived in Perth and she and her family were going back to Hungary and wanted a good car. Our Golf was in really good condition and they paid good money for it. Usually when people in the motel found out that you were leaving, they knew that you would have to sell your things and would try and buy them for a low price. They would wait for the last moment because they knew that you would either sell it for peanuts or just leave it there. We bought a really old bomb, a Citroen to have while we waited and we managed to sell that too before we left. It didn't matter about the price as it was very cheap when we bought it. We also got rid of the TV and everything else too. The family at home was really nervous as we were going so far away.

The night before we left we had to pack everything up and be organised as we had to leave at about 4am the next morning. Because it was early September the mornings were really chilly. We had collected a few little things and had to sit on our luggage to make it shut. One of the suitcases wouldn't shut and we had to put a belt around it to close it. Whilst we were living in Altmunstern Laszlo had made a Samurai Sword. He already had a blade and went searching in the forest for the right wood. He found what he was looking for and made carvings on it. The catana was really well made; it was the right size and all. The whole thing was just beautiful and when we were packing we took it apart, so that it would just look like bits and pieces, not like a real catana. We were a bit concerned that they might not let us through customs with it, that maybe they would think we might try and attack people with it. We couldn't believe that it was our last night in Almunstern; it was a really strange feeling. We were up very early the next morning and were soon ready to go.

There were about five other families, some Hungarian and others not, who were also travelling with us. Most people had friends or family to say goodbye to, but my brother and his wife didn't come down. We felt a bit alone as we left. We couldn't understand how they wouldn't come and say goodbye when we were going to the other side of the world and didn't know if we would ever see them again. It was very sad for me but we couldn't change anything.

Chapter Six

The bus took us to Vienna. They took us to Traiskirchen again and we had to put our entire luggage in the basement as we needed to go to the Australian Embassy in Vienna. We were transported there and had to go in and sit around a big table. We were given a passport and a visa. We really wanted to go to Brisbane or the Sunshine Coast or somewhere like that. The choices we were given were Brisbane,

Sydney, Melbourne or Perth. When we got given our visas whatever was written on it was where we had to go. When we got our visa and it said Melbourne, we were momentarily a bit disappointed. However this soon faded because at least we were still getting the chance to go. We and one of the other families (who were going to Brisbane) were given a booklet. I don't know why only two of us were given it, but inside it said that somebody would be waiting for us at the airport and also that a house was being rented out for us with some basic furniture in it. Plus the fridge would have food in it. This sounded too good to be true and we were very happy. After being given that booklet we had to sign more papers and then we were free to go. The bus would come and pick us up at Traiskirchen the next day to take us to the airport. We didn't want to stay in Traiskirchen for another night so we went back and found the little hotel near the church that we had stayed in when we first arrived in Vienna. One of the rooms was free so we could spend our last night there. We had a beautiful dinner and it was a very interesting feeling to go back there. The first time we didn't know what lay ahead and now we knew that we were free to go to Australia. It was quite an amazing feeling. We were just so happy.

The next morning we went back to Traiskirchen to collect our luggage. We had to borrow a belt from somebody to keep it closed, as it was really starting to fall apart at that stage. I couldn't help but think that we looked like stereotypical poor immigrants whose suitcases wouldn't close! The double decker bus picked us up and took us to the airport, which was quite a long journey. A few months before there had been some kind of shooting incident at Vienna airport, so it was full of soldiers and German Shepherd dogs. Everybody was also really tense and we hoped that nothing else would happen while we were there. Fortunately nothing did, we just checked in our luggage and were soon ready to board the plane. First we flew to Frankfurt and then we had to wait there for four hours for our connecting flight. It was quite late at night and the kids were really tired. After Frankfurt we flew into Bangkok, where we got a QANTAS sticker to identify which flight we were on. When we got off the plane in Bangkok we had to walk down the steps and across the terminal. We couldn't believe how hot and humid it was. At first we thought that it must have been the heat from the plane's engine but as we kept walking we realised that the heat stayed with us. We had never experienced that kind of heat before in Europe. It was about 33C° but the humidity was about 90%. It was almost unbearable for us and we were so relieved to get inside the air-conditioned airport terminal. We were hoping that Australia would not be that hot or we didn't know what we would do. We didn't have much time so we just had a quick look around before getting back on the plane. After Bangkok we flew into Singapore and just as we were about to land Anita got sick. She was using the sick bags and I tried to take her into the bathroom but because we were landing we weren't allowed to leave our seats.

I just held the bag and hoped that she wouldn't need another one. Fortunately she didn't and when we landed I had to quickly find somewhere to get rid of the bag.

We thought that Singapore was just beautiful, even though we didn't get the opportunity to even leave the airport. There were lots of different shops and everything was clean. We just walked around and enjoyed the surrounds. Before we had to board again Anita said to me that she didn't want to go any further. She had had enough of flying and thought that she would be sick again when she got back on the plane. I explained that we were almost there and we couldn't stay in Singapore anyway. When we got on the plane I asked the Stewardess for some medication for her. Fortunately she went straight to sleep so that made things much easier. When we had been in Austria Laszlo had known a little bit of German and I knew a little bit of English, so now that we were on a flight that spoke English, Laszlo said to me that now it was my turn to do the communicating. When they came around and asked us if we wanted a drink, he said to ask for whiskey and ice. I thought that was simple enough and each time they came around I asked for whiskey with ice. I think that the stewardess must have thought that I was a real drunken sailor because I kept asking for so much whiskey!

Soon it was almost time to land in Melbourne and they came around and gave us the necessary papers to fill out, asking if we had anything to declare and other such questions. There was a man there to assist non-English speaking people and he was very helpful. Laszlo thought that we had better put down the Japanese Catana sword, just to be on the safe side. We didn't want to get pulled up later for not declaring it. Just after we landed the stewardess sprayed the whole cabin. They explained that Australia was a big island that wasn't exposed to a lot of different germs, so they had to try and keep it free of different diseases.

When the plane had actually landed we were so excited and happy. We were looking out the windows, trying to see what we could. There was a whole new world waiting for us in this new country and as far as we knew somebody would be waiting for us and we had a home to go to. After we collected our luggage we were queuing for customs clearance when we heard our name being called over the loudspeaker. So we came forward and they asked us to go to a different table with our entire luggage. We were really nervous and when we got over there they asked us where the Japanese sword was. We then had to remember where we had packed it! Because we had packed the different pieces in different cases, it took us a while to find the whole sword! They then asked Laszlo to put it together and they took it and looked at it closely. Then they asked us who made it and Laszlo replied that he had made it. They were really impressed; they were admiring it and saying how beautiful it was. They even showed one of the other guys who worked there. They were so friendly; they then helped us to take it apart and also helped us to close our luggage up again. They then stamped our passports and let us through.

After we got through the gate we were waiting for the person who was supposed to meet us. We weren't too concerned at first; we thought that maybe they were just late. We were so lucky going through customs because the other people we knew had everything searched. They had to unpack books and just about everything that you could possibly think of. We waited for quite some time and got talking to a nice Hungarian priest. We showed him the booklet that we had received back in Vienna and he said that he had never heard of anything like that before. Finally, after about an hour and a half, all the other Hungarian families had finally passed through customs. There were eight families all together. We were still waiting and nobody had shown up to meet us. The priest then said to us that we were free to do whatever we wanted, but he was there to take the other Hungarian families to a hostel in Maribyrnong. We could go with them if we wanted to and he would arrange accommodation for us or we could stay and wait for this other person who was supposed to meet us. We didn't know what to do but we knew that we didn't want to go to another hostel again after spending about 5½ months living like that in Austria. We just wanted to get our own place and start our new life straight away. On the other hand we didn't have much choice, because we couldn't speak the language and we really didn't know anything about this city. We thanked the priest and went with him and the other families to the hostel. When we got off the bus the first thing we noticed was the colour of the sky. It was the most gorgeous blue we had never seen anything like it before in our lives. We were just amazed the air was really fresh and clear as well. It's these little things that tend to stick in your mind. Maribyrnong itself was not very attractive and the streets were a bit dirty but we were just glad to be there.

When we got to the hostel Laszlo said that we weren't going in. He went into the office and tried to find out what was going on. Nobody had heard about this kind of arrangement before and they didn't seem to know who this person was. Neither of us really wanted to go in because we didn't want to get stuck there. We just wanted to get things started. About half an hour later Laszlo came back outside and said that we didn't really have much option. We would have to go inside and stay there for a little while until we could sort something out. The hostel had one main building with a big eatery and around it lots of smaller buildings, which were two levels. There were four little units in each building. We had a unit that had two bedrooms and one bathroom. Once we were settled in, the kids and I went to sleep because we were so tired and jet-lagged. Laszlo, however couldn't sleep, so he said that he would go for a walk around to find out exactly where we were and what was going on. When Laszlo set out for his walk, there weren't any people on the street but there was a big black and white bird that was jumping alongside him. It was basically following him along the top of the fence. Laszlo didn't know what was going on and all he could remember was the Hitchcock film 'The Birds', which was a bit of a scary thought. He was a bit concerned but didn't realise at the time that it was a Magpie and that it was nesting season. It just kept following him but didn't attack him, fortunately.

Finally Laszlo reached a shopping centre. To him it was just huge; he had never seen anything like it before. So he went inside and decided to have a look around the supermarket to perhaps buy us some food. He went to get a shopping trolley and tried to pull it out of its holder, but they were all chained together and he couldn't free it from the others. He didn't know what to do and was getting very frustrated trying to pull the trolley out. It made a real noise and the young checkout operator looked up as if to say, 'oh, it looks like another recent immigrant has arrived into Melbourne. There must have been a plane load!' She showed him that if you put 20c into the machine then you could release one of the trolleys. This was definitely an interesting first experience for Laszlo in our new country. As he walked around he was just amazed at the huge range of things there were to buy and knew that we had made a good choice in coming to Australia. He bought some fresh rolls and some ham and came back. We had decided not to unpack because we didn't think that we would be there for very long, we were hopeful that this man would show up and take us to our house.

When we were looking around the complex to find out where we had to eat, we saw that there was a place where you could collect mail. On the first day that we were there one of the other people came up to us and said that we had some mail. We were dumbfounded and asked how we could possibly have mail sent to us when nobody knew where we were. We hadn't known ourselves where we would end up, we knew it was Melbourne but we didn't have an address. So how could anybody possibly have sent mail that arrived before we did? We were sure that it must have been a mistake. But when we checked it out we found that it was for us. It was from my sister in law in Austria. I almost had a heart attack when I saw it. We hadn't spoken to them for eight weeks before we left Austria, they had spat on us and hadn't come to say goodbye to us when we left. So why were they sending us a letter? We opened it quickly and read it. My sister in law was asking us to sponsor them to get to Australia. For some reason they apparently had no chance to come here, unless they could get someone to sponsor them. That meant that they might have to remain in Austria or worse still, might have to go back to Hungary.

We read and reread the letter several times and couldn't help but think that life was very interesting sometimes. They had treated us so badly but now when we were the only people who could help them they were being nice to us again. I thought about the whole situation for a very long time and pondered what I should do.

Anita and me in 1980 at home.

Laszlo and Anita get along from
the first time.

Our wedding day on
24th of April 1982

Our house and our car the Trabant

On the way back from Norway.

I never can ask for best daughters!

Four generations at Christmas time.

Laszlo's parents.

We are very proud of our new Lada car!

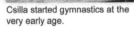

Csilla started gymnastics at the
very early age.

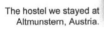

The hostel we stayed at
Altmunstern, Austria.

Say good bye from my dad at the station.

Our first Christmas in Australia.

Happy Christmas with Jack.

Eventually I sat down and wrote a long letter in reply. I explained to them that although we didn't want to bring up the past, they had put us through a terrible ordeal that we didn't deserve. I talked about the things that they had done and how it had affected us. I said that I would help almost any other person who wanted to be sponsored, even somebody that I had never met, but not them. So if that meant that they had to stay in Austria or go back to Hungary then that was their bad luck. We then posted the letter back to them and didn't hear from them about it again. After I had written the letter I felt a kind of sense of relief. Maybe it seems nasty but I guess I felt a kind of revenge as well. I thought that maybe now that they would understand how we felt when they abandoned us. I don't think that they ever really understood just what they did to us.

That night we went and had some dinner and most people went to sleep except for those who had arrived on the plane with us. By looking around the building and seeing the lights in the windows, you could work out who was still awake, which meant that they had been on the same flight. Jet-lag had really hit us and it took us a few days to recover.

The next day a man came to see us. It turned out that he was the one who was supposed to pick us up at the airport. The trouble was that he didn't have a car, which was why he hadn't arrived. But it turned out he would have probably only taken us to this hostel anyway. The booklet that said there was a house waiting for us was untrue. He had never seen anything like that before and had no idea who had set the whole thing up or how we had come to get that booklet. After chatting for a while he then asked us what our plans were. We said that we would like to buy a house and his eyes just widened in shock. He said, "You can't do that!" We answered "Why not? Don't people in Australia buy houses?" He said, "Yes of course they do but you have just arrived. How much money do you have?" We didn't want to tell him, of course, because it wasn't really any of his business; we just said that we didn't have an awful lot but maybe enough for a deposit on a house. He said that as we had just arrived we should wait for a while and get settled and then think about a house. We really didn't want to stay there though, we wanted to get on with things – find a job and somewhere to live. We had already spent 5 ½ months waiting in Austria and we didn't want to waste any more time. We didn't want to collect the dole, we were ready and willing to get jobs and work hard. He said we didn't have to be in such a rush.

I didn't go to lunch that day, as I didn't feel like anything but when Laszlo came back, he said, "You won't believe who I saw." It turned out that the tiny little boy who had captivated us at Traiskirchen was here as well. It was an incredible coincidence; we couldn't believe it. We hadn't had any contact with them since Traiskirchen and now we had ended up in the same city, in the same building! We went to see the family and found out that they were actually living above us. The wife came down to see us and asked why we hadn't unpacked. I said that we really didn't want to stay there. She just laughed and said they had said the same thing when they arrived but they had now been there for three weeks, so it was best if she just helped me unpack. We had a bit of a laugh about it and she gave me a hand with the unpacking.

After we settled in a bit, we had the opportunity to register for Medicare and to open an account at the Commonwealth Bank. There was a woman who helped us fill in paper work as well as finding a school for the girls. When we showed her the paper that we had gotten in Vienna she said that she hadn't seen anything like it before. Then she called over another man and he said that he had heard something about it. Apparently some people were conducting an experiment to see how immigrants coped when they first arrive. There were no houses, howeve that was all a lie. We were really stunned by that and thought that it was an awful thing to do. But we said that we were coping very well.

Before we had left Austria we didn't have a problem changing our Hungarian currency to Austrian shillings. Because we didn't know where we would end up we decided to change all our money to shillings and then we could exchange it when we arrived. We had also been lucky to sell some of our jewellery to the nice couple that Laszlo worked for and this also gave us a bit of extra cash, as they gave us a good price. When we arrived in Australia and converted the cash we had it came to $10,000.-. One day not long after we arrived we were going to the shopping centre and saw a car yard close by with an old looking white Ford Falcon advertised for $9,999-. We couldn't believe it. I said to Laszlo that we had sold our beautiful home in Hungary but all we would be able to get with the proceeds was an old Falcon car. For a moment it seemed like we wouldn't have much hope at all and we were worried.

We didn't let it worry us *too* much though; instead we made some plans. We wanted to buy a map first, so we went to a shopping centre and bought a Melway. The next thing we wanted was to buy a car, hopefully much cheaper than the Falcon that we had seen. Laszlo talked to some people who had been there a while to find out where to get a car. We ended up buying a little yellow Toyota station wagon for $3,000.-. The next thing we wanted to buy was a HiFi and a TV. It's interesting to see our priorities were high for a TV, but it was something that we thought we needed. Soon after we had made these purchases we found out that a man came to visit the hostel from the Hungarian Community Centre in Wantirna. We thought it would be an idea to go and visit this community centre, so we looked at the map and worked out how to get there. We went there one night and introduced ourselves. We were hoping that somebody might be able to help us with getting a job or finding somewhere to live. I was wearing my leather skirt, which was very fashionable at the time. When we arrived everybody looked at us in surprise and asked us how we had gotten there, as it was across on the other side of the city. When we explained that we had driven a car, they asked us where we got a car and we explained that we had bought it. They couldn't believe it and asked us how long we had been in Australia. We said two weeks and they were shocked that we had gotten a car so fast. We couldn't work out what the big deal was. They were also surprised at how well dressed we were. I don't know what they expected we should have worn. After that they asked us if we wanted to watch some films and we said OK, just to be polite. We then went into a room with quite a lot of older people. It turned out that they were watching black and white slides. Everybody else was so excited about watching these black and white slides but we didn't know what the big deal was. Csilla was about five then and she turned to me and said, 'why aren't they moving Mum?' After that everybody just looked at us. I think they must have been thinking 'who are these people and what are they doing here?' After that we just left and decided that the Hungarian Community Centre was not for us!

We asked this man if he could help us find a place to rent. Of course we didn't have any idea where a good area was to live but he said he could come and see us in a few days. We found out also that we could go to the language school there. We were still looking for jobs but it was difficult without knowing the language. It was difficult to even read the paper. One day one of the other Hungarian people asked us if we wanted to go out with them to a gathering that one of the priests was organising. It was apparently with Hungarian immigrants who had arrived back in the 1950s and were still living in Melbourne. Each of these couples would then come and take a family with them and would show them around, have lunch together and talk about how we were finding things since arriving. We agreed to do this because we hardly knew anybody and it was good to have somebody to drive us around and show us what were nice areas and things like that. We also wouldn't have a language problem. Maribyrnong was all right, but we didn't really like that area too much and were hoping to find somewhere a bit nicer.

One Sunday morning we went down to the car park and there were a lot of cars on the other side, each one with a man standing next to it. We looked at each other and said that it was almost like a cattle sale and these men were sizing up who looked like the best couple to take with them! It was a weird feeling, we almost felt like we really were up for sale. Eventually one guy chose us, he said his name was George and invited us to come into his car with him. He seemed really nice so we thought we would go along with him. He had a nice car and we found him really easy to talk to. We went with him to Glen Waverley where he and his wife Cecilia lived in a nice house. When we drove across to the eastern side of Melbourne, we started to appreciate that it really was a beautiful city. There were lots of trees and pretty little houses with nice wide streets and we decided that this was the area that we wanted to find a house in. We felt like we had known George and Cecilia for a long time and found them very easy to get along with. Cecilia was cooking us a beautiful meal for lunch, so we felt quite at home. After lunch they took us to the church to listen to the priest speak. We weren't religious but decided that we would go along, it wasn't a hardship after they had been so hospitable to us.

At the church we met all the other couples and went inside to listen to the priest speak. It wasn't too bad really. After it was finished we talked a little bit more and went back to their house again. They explained to us that it was the first time that they had done this as well, so it was a new experience for all of. Then Cecilia asked if we were going to go to the church every Sunday and we explained that we weren't religious. She then said that we should have told them that because they weren't religious either and hardly ever went to church themselves. We could have just skipped that part of the day and gone somewhere else! This was quite an icebreaker and we felt even more comfortable in their company after that. We had a wonderful afternoon, we laughed a lot and the food was just lovely. I found out that Cecilia had worked for some cafés and restaurants, so she was a very good cook. It was wonderful to have such nice food after some of the strange meals we had had since leaving Hungary. The food in Austria was always very good but it was prepared for large groups of people. This lunch, however, was a real home cooked meal and we appreciated every single bite. We took their address and phone number and they invited us to come back whenever we wanted to or to call. They really liked the kids and us too; they felt like they were grandparents to them.

When the old man who was going to help us find somewhere to live came around, we told him that we definitely wanted to live in the Eastern suburbs. It turned out that he knew a real estate agent in Box Hill. We drove him over there and explained what we were looking for and what our limit was. They had a two bedroom house that was close to the primary school and close to the bus stop. There were some others, as well but this seemed like the best one. The agent gave us the street name and the house number and we went to go and see it. We found it and tried to go into the house but the key didn't work. We tried to look in through the windows and thought that it wasn't bad at all, although we were very surprised to see that there was furniture inside. We didn't think that it was furnished because the agent hadn't mentioned it. We then went back to the agency and explained that the key hadn't worked. The woman said not to worry, that she would come out with us, so we went back there and tried to go back into the house again. The woman (who had been in her own car) waved to us from the next house and said that it was the rental property. We had been trying to get into the wrong house! It was a nice clean house and they had an above ground swimming pool in the backyard. We decided that we would take it, even though the pool was very green and dirty at the time. Feeling excited, we went back to the real estate agency and signed the necessary papers and paid the bond and two weeks rent (it was $140 per week).

Chapter Seven

We went back to Maribyrnong and gathered
our friends together to tell them our news. We
then packed our car up - although at that stage
we really didn't have very much to pack – and
moved into our house. That same man took us
to the Salvation Army and helped us to choose
a table, some chairs and some beds for the
girls. They also gave us a $30 food voucher,
which we thought was really nice. We then
went to a second hand shop and bought a very

old fridge and washing machine.   Then we went to the shopping centre to find Telecom to get our phone connected.   While we were there, the man we were with met another old Hungarian man who was a friend of his.   We explained that we had just arrived in the country five weeks ago and were settling in to our house.   We also explained that Laszlo was looking for a job and the man asked what his qualifications were.   When we said that he was an electrician, this man said that one of his friends was looking for an electrician.   We thought that this was a wonderful coincidence and he also offered us a bed that he had.   It was only basic furniture at that time, but it was enough to start with.

After we had picked up the bed we went shopping for some food to fill up the fridge.

For our first meal there I thought that I would make chicken and fried potatoes.   The chicken was done and I put the potatoes in the hot oil to cook.   It was only then that I realised that we didn't have anything to take them out with.   We only had basic cutlery – knives, forks and spoons. The chips were starting to get darker and darker and eventually I managed to fish them out with two forks held together. But it made me realise that you just don't think about how many things you really need when you set up a new house. You usually think of the big things, but not about all the small things. When you've had everything that you need before, you don't often think about starting again, but it worked out fine in the end and we had a nice meal after all.

After we had been in the house for a little while, randomly a man knocked on the door. He looked Greek and could hardly speak any English either. I worked out that he wanted to mow the lawn. I asked him how much it would cost. He replied that he didn't want any money; he just wanted to mow the lawn. I called Laszlo over and explained that this man wanted to mow the lawn for free, which seemed like a pretty strange thing. Eventually we worked out that he was the owner of the house and that he was happy to come and mow the lawn for us. We had assumed that as the tenants we would have to do the mowing, but we didn't mind at all. He seemed very happy to do it and was a nice man. After that first time he used to bring his wife with him and she would come in and have a cup of coffee with me and we would always have a good chat. It was a very inventive conversation though because she was Greek and only had very limited English, and I had almost no English at all. We had to use lots of sign language but we managed quite well! They were both really nice, friendly people.

Not too long after we moved in to our house in Box Hill we decided to clean the pool. We asked the owners and they agreed, so we spent a bit of time scrubbing and cleaning and filled it up again with fresh water. We had to spend a bit of money on it and it did require some maintenance, but it was definitely worth it. People had said that living in Melbourne we wouldn't have much use for a pool, but we used it a lot and got a huge amount of enjoyment out of it. We would also invite the neighbours over to swim in it as well. At first the neighbour's kids used to hang over the fence when they saw us swimming and asked if they could come over. They were really nice, friendly people and we had a lot of fun with them in the pool.

Laszlo went to see the man about the job and he got it, however it wasn't an electrician's job; it was actually working with air-conditioners. He didn't really know much about them at all, but this man was happy to help and for him to have the job. We were elated that we were going to be earning money again. By this stage it was getting close to Christmas.

Laszlo soon settled into his new job and before long it was time for Anita to go to school. There was a primary school close by, which was very handy. They put Anita into grade four even though she couldn't speak English. She was put into a normal class. It was very interesting to see how fast children can learn. After about three weeks she could speak with her friends in English. The teachers went with her and showed her all the little shops around

the school and explained what they all were –
things like the hairdresser and the fish and
chips shop. They tried to explain to her what
everything was; they were really very helpful.
Children really do pick up languages much
faster; it was definitely harder for us. Our next
door neighbours were really friendly and
helpful as well. They were Australian and had
children that were similar ages to ours. I used
to go over when I got the school newsletter
because I couldn't understand what it said and
she would spend ages explaining what
everything meant. I will always remember
once when they had to take an apron to school.
I didn't know what an apron was, I did have a
dictionary but it was very difficult to translate
the whole newsletter word by word. Even so,
sometimes the translation wouldn't make sense
anyway. Fortunately my neighbour explained
what an apron was. I really struggled with
English at first, but because I had to take Anita
to school and do the shopping and go to the
bank and other things like that, I learned ways

to communicate. Slowly some words and sentences started making sense.

About two months after we moved into our house at Box Hill the old man who was supposed to pick us up at the airport, rang me and asked if I was going to pick my brother up. I asked him what he was talking about and he explained that my brother and his family were arriving in Melbourne that day. I hadn't known anything about this and was very surprised but I said that we wouldn't be picking them up. He said that in that case he would have to go to greet them. How they managed to get here I'm not sure. I don't know if their situation changed or they managed to get somebody to sponsor them. In any case they hadn't told us about it, however, we did know that they were now here. They apparently found somewhere to rent, but I really didn't care at that point.

After a few weeks my younger niece rang me. She said, 'Guess where we are?' I told her that I knew they had arrived. She was surprised to hear this as they obviously thought that we hadn't found out. In any case she wanted to come and see us and I said that was all right, we would come and pick her up if she wanted. We drove over and picked up my two nieces and bought them back to our house. The kids were really happy to see each other again and I was happy to see them too. They continued to visit and we took our kids to their place, although we never spoke to my brother and his wife. We would just drop the girls off or they would drop their girls off. They would stop a few houses away and we would do the same, so we didn't even actually see them. This situation went on for quite a while.

I found out that there was a language school quite close to where we lived and if you were an immigrant then you could go there for free for a year. I applied to go and found out that the next course started in February. This worked out well for us because Csilla would be starting school at the same time and I would be able to go while the girls were at school. It was harder for Laszlo because he didn't have as many opportunities to learn the language. He was working with a Hungarian guy and didn't come into contact with as many people as I did during the day. He did ask the man he worked for to speak English and he tried to pronounce some of the words. But his boss wasn't very helpful, he said that he couldn't understand Laszlo and told him to just speak in Hungarian instead. For me however, it was really necessary to have some knowledge of English if I wanted to get most of my day-to-day things done.

We spent our first Christmas with our friends George and Cecilia and we had a wonderful time. They were always so hospitable and helpful and treated us like family. They were really guiding us through any obstacles that we faced.

Soon enough the summer holidays were finished and it was time for the kids to go to school. The language school was from 9-12 each morning and first off Csilla would finish at noon as well. They didn't do the whole day until later in the year. Csilla's teachers knew that I was at the language school, so they would look after Csilla for that extra time each day, until I could come and get her. This was very nice of them. After three months at school that year, Anita was first in her class for English and spelling and Csilla's language was almost perfect as well. It was quite amazing that they could pick it up so fast. They would have conversations in English at home and we would just look at another and wonder what was going on. It seemed so weird that we couldn't understand our own kids!

On my first day at the language school the teacher gave us a piece of paper with a short story on it that we were supposed to analyse and understand. We weren't allowed to use our dictionaries either. I really concentrated and tried very hard to understand what it said. But all I could understand was that they had taken someone's heart and had put it in one town and had then put their skin in the next town and the skeleton was somewhere else! I just looked around and wondered what on earth they were talking about. It seemed that everybody else knew what was going on, as nobody was asking questions. This seemed a bit strange, because it was a beginner's English class, so that should have meant that nobody there was able to speak English. The lesson was soon over but I still couldn't understand at all what the story was about. Who was this person whose skin was somewhere and whose heart was somewhere else - it just seemed so strange. I then went home and decided to go through the dictionary and translate every word. It took a really long time but I did it because I wanted to work out what they were talking about. Eventually I worked out that they were talking about a horse! I had never heard of Phar Lap before, so that was why I had no clue what they were talking about. I asked my friends and they explained that Phar Lap had been a famous racehorse who won the Melbourne Cup in 1930 and was a real legend. His skeleton lives in the National Museum in Wellington, and his stuffed and mounted hide is in the National Museum in Melbourne. I was just glad to find out that it wasn't a person that they were A few days later a Hungarian interpreter came. There were many different nationalities in the class. Some were from Mexico, some from Cuba, some from Poland as well as many other places. There weren't any other Hungarians but there were a lot of Chinese. This interpreter asked me if I was happy with the class and I explained that I didn't think I was in the right class because I just didn't understand anything at all. I explained that it seemed like everybody else knew what was going on but I didn't. She then talked to the teacher and the teacher talked to the other interpreters and it turned out that we were all in the same boat! Nobody understood the work but they all thought that everybody else in the class did. The teacher was quite happy to discover what level we were on. She had talked to us in English, but she didn't really know how much of it we understood. Because everybody was nodding, she assumed that we understood what she said, but in reality nobody really knew what was going on. She went back to basics again and turned out to be a wonderful teacher.

She explained everything to us and we didn't
even need our dictionaries most of the time.
We would have role plays where one of us
would be the shop assistant and the other
would be a customer trying to buy something.
This kind of thing was quite helpful, as it was
the that we could come across every day. We
also learned how to speak on the phone, rather
than just saying hello, we should say 'Hello,
how are you?'. Then we got into conversations
and more complex things. We really learned a
lot in the six months, it was just amazing. On
our last day we got some money together and
bought our teacher a present. I was the one
who was chosen to give it to her and who had
to say some nice words about her and how
much we appreciated everything that she had
done and how much fun we had during the
course. All in all it was a very positive
experience and I was so proud that the class
had chosen me as the spokesperson. The
teacher then said to me that for the first few
days I hadn't said a word but now they couldn't
shut me up! Everybody was laughing. We had

become like a big family, we had even been on an excursion to the zoo. It was great when we could all speak some English because it meant that we could find out where each other was from, some of their background and about their families. The kids were also doing really well at school, so we were all settling well into our new life. I also used to watch a lot of TV to help me with my English. It's amazing how quiz shows, like Wheel Of Fortune, can help you to learn English. I watched everything because it all helped me. I also tried to read newspapers and at the end of the six months I could read reasonably well. I could also follow films and TV shows. Even if you couldn't understand every word you could work it out by the rest of the story. At the end of the six months my speaking, reading and comprehension was OK but I found the writing, grammar and spelling very difficult. So I applied for another six months in the school but because there were so many other immigrants wanting to go there, I wasn't allowed to go back. They said that because my speaking was quite good, that was it for me.

After I finished language school, I said to Laszlo that I would like to start applying for jobs. I took our papers to a government office and tried to explain that I would like our qualifications accepted in Australia. We found out that Laszlo would have to start all over again. He would have to go back to school to get an electrician's licence (P and B licence) and then he would have to work with an electrician for a few years before he could get an A Electrician's licence. The funny thing was that he was a Master Electrician back in Hungary. We realised that there were different rules all over the world regarding electricity, but the job itself was quite similar. Even if they had had a one year course where he could have learnt all the different Australian rules, it would have made a big difference. It seemed unfair that he had to go through all that again. He did actually get the P licence but decided that he would not go any further because the language was very difficult for him. He didn't get any practice and it was a real struggle for him to grasp English. His practical experience was perfect but the written test was extremely difficult. He decided that he would keep working for his boss and would see where that took him. I started looking for a job as a tracer or a draftsperson. When we went to the city to see if they would accept my qualifications I found out that they meant absolutely nothing here also. This was a real blow for me as I had studied hard in Hungary to earn my qualification to design and draw houses. I felt very crushed when I found this out, as it meant that all my hard work had been for nothing, however. There was little that I could do.

Through some Hungarian friends I found out that there was a Hungarian architect close to where we lived and I thought that maybe he could help me. I went to see him and explained what was going on. He said that I could come to his place and trace his drawings, but he wouldn't be able to pay me. I didn't mind this really; as I could keep a copy of the drawings I did and take them with me when I applied for other jobs. He also gave me a reference that I had worked for him. We talked quite a lot and he understood what I was going through. They told me that if I want my qualification, I would have to go to the RMIT to complete a four year degree. This I was not prepared to do, as the girls were still so young. I simply kept looking through the papers for drafting jobs.

I hadn't really driven much since we arrived. We only had the one car and it was a scary thought to try and drive on the other side of the road. After three months we needed to do a written driving licence test. We got the book and I translated the whole thing and we tried to study the best we could. The signs here in Australia are much simpler than those in Europe, so we could follow them OK. We were able to complete this test as we were allowed an interpreter. An old guy came with us. We went into the room and got some forms. We went in together but they kept someone watching over us so we wouldn't cheat. We didn't really want to cheat anyway; we didn't see much point in that. This old fellow was supposed to translate the questions for us and tell us what the possible answers were, then we would have to answer separately. Some of the questions were quite obvious but some of them didn't make sense after translation. This was really puzzling and we looked at each other as if to say, 'What now? We said to him that maybe he didn't translate the question or the answers properly and we went through them again. He said that they were very difficult questions to translate and he felt bad that he was supposed to be helping us but instead we were quite confused. We did, however, pass the test, and that was the main thing in the end. There was one question that we got wrong, concerning the blood alcohol limit. We didn't have to have a driving test back then, which was a relief. We were issued with our Victorian drivers licence.

Laszlo was still working for the same guy and one Friday this man arrived at our place and said to me, 'don't have a heart attack.' I thought that he meant that I was surprised that they had shown up, that maybe Laszlo was supposed to have told me they were coming and didn't. But I said that was OK and invited him in. Laszlo then followed and I could see that his hand was in thick bandages – I almost did have a heart attack then! I asked what had happened. This guy had a little workshop in his back yard that had an electric guillotine. Laszlo was supposed to be manufacturing some metal ductwork and he had to put metal sheets in this guillotine. Laszlo had left two of his fingers near the guard that kept the metal in place and this metal guard had jammed against his fingers and had taken a piece off the top. Laszlo always fainted at the sight of his own blood. He was fine when it was somebody else, but not himself. He could feel himself fainting, but couldn't do anything about it. When they found him he was lying on the floor bleeding, with the tops of two of his fingers missing. They took him to the hospital, but they couldn't sew the tops of his fingers back on again. They bandaged everything up and said that he should be OK, as he hadn't damaged the bone at all. It healed well and you can't even notice now which fingers were injured. He was in a lot of pain for a little while though. He went back to work not too long after that. It was a very harrowing experience at the time though.

As time went on Laszlo became more frustrated at not being able to speak the language. He arranged with his employer to work half days and enrolled at the language school so he could get a better grip on English. He did this for two months. It was harder to live on half wages but we managed and it was worth it for Laszlo to be able to improve his English skills.

We had quite a few Hungarian friends and one day we invited some of them to come over for Sunday lunch. They were still living in Maribyrnong and Laszlo went over to pick them up. Whilst I was waiting for them to arrive I got a phone call. Laszlo had been in a car accident on his way to pick them up. He had accidentally gone through a red light and a car had hit him on the passenger side. The car was a bit damaged but fortunately Laszlo was fine. He had been preoccupied while he was driving as we had experienced so many changes in a short time and it had affected his concentration. It was a big responsibility for him to look after us in this whole new life and it was quite stressful at times. Our friends did eventually arrive for lunch and we had a nice time with them. We were able to fix the car at home too, so it didn't turn out too bad in the end.

I was still looking for jobs but wasn't having much success. I applied everywhere I could think of. If I applied to a big firm, they said that I would be better off at a smaller architecture firm as they would be able to pay more attention to me. But then when I applied to a smaller place, they looked at my drawings and said that they were very good but because I didn't have any Australian experience, I would be better off at a bigger firm, as they could offer me more individual attention! It seemed like I couldn't win. For the first two years that we lived in Australia I applied for countless jobs in drafting and went to numerous interviews, but something was always wrong. There was constantly a reason or an excuse as to why I couldn't be offered the job. They all admired my drawings and said how good they were but none would give me an exact reason why I couldn't work for them. After two years I got sick of the whole situation and went to an employment agency where I applied for jobs cleaning houses. That was what I did to earn some money. I was still frustrated at not being able to use my skills, but didn't have any other option. I wasn't prepared to go to university for four years and besides I knew that my English wasn't good enough to allow me to study at tertiary level. All my Hungarian friends said that I just needed to find the right person, who had the right contacts to get me a job. But I could never find that 'right' person. I had been to almost every drafting office in Melbourne and none of them were the 'right' person.

We continued to meet other Hungarian people in Melbourne. George and Cecilia took us to a Hungarian house and introduced us to some of the people there. We did meet some friendly people and it was nice to socialise, but we found out that it wasn't really our scene. A lot of the women there tended to be very competitive and would be jealous if somebody was wearing nicer clothes than they were. Some of them would wear fake jewellery so they looked more important and wealthy. They would never wear the same dress twice because they were so concerned about what other people would think. We really didn't like the competitive attitude they had. They would always ask how much Laszlo earned or how much money we had and would want to know everything that we were doing. I thought that it was rude to ask such personal questions, but that is what some Hungarian people do – they always like to know everybody else's business. One day one of the old men tried to sell Laszlo a little badge with the Hungarian flag. Laszlo said 'No thanks", he didn't want to put one on. The man replied that Laszlo wasn't a real Hungarian if he wouldn't wear the badge. Laszlo replied that he was Hungarian inside – that he was proud of it and didn't lie about it – but he didn't think that he needed to show it on the outside. All in all we reduced our visits as it was something that we didn't really want to belong to. I also couldn't understand why, people who came out from Hungary, would created their own Hungarian community in they new country. They found a Hungarian butcher, a Hungarian hairdresser and so on. Some of them didn't even want to learn the language or live like people here. I always thought that we chose to come here, we applied for a visa and that we should be thankful that the government let us come. It wasn't up to the Australian people to learn Hungarian just because we had arrived, it was up to us to learn English and communicate with other Australians. The country wasn't going to change just because we were here; it was up to us to live like other Australians. This didn't mean that we couldn't have Hungarian friends or shouldn't enjoy Hungarian cooking, rather that we should experience both cultures. I had many Australian friends as well as friends from other nationalities. We decided on the friends that we wanted to keep from the Hungarian community and spent less and less time there and gradually lost contact with the people that we didn't want to stay friends with anymore.

We found a judo club for Laszlo and he spent a fair bit of time there. I wasn't too happy about this sometimes because it was difficult for me as I didn't have a car and was home with the kids all day. One day after he came home from work I suggested that we should go and see some friends of ours but he said that he was really tired, so I didn't push. However after dinner he got a phone call from one of the guys at the judo club who wanted him to go and train with them. He was packed and gone in a few minutes. This made me quite annoyed and I felt isolated because I didn't have the car and couldn't go anywhere. It felt like judo was more important than doing something with us. He was able to interact with people at work and could then have fun with his judo friends, whereas I didn't have another adult to talk to when I was at home and had to rely on public transport if I wanted to go out. When I suggested that we do something he would always say that he was too tired, but if it was judo then he was all right again. This made me feel unhappy and I cried about it a lot, although I never really told Laszlo how I felt because I didn't want to upset him. Back then we weren't always great at communicating with each other if we had problems.

On one occasion the judo club asked him to go away for a competition, which was going to last a few days. Finally I snapped and decided to speak my mind. I said that he couldn't go. When I think about it now, it was because I wanted to be with him not because I didn't want him to have fun and enjoy his judo. I was upset that he never asked me to go with him. He just assumed that I didn't want to go or that we wouldn't be able to find anybody else to look after the kids. We didn't have Grandma and Grandpa to do that any more, but George and Cecilia were more than happy to, we just never asked them. I guess he thought that because I was the mother, I should mind the kids and as he was the man, he was allowed to go out and have fun. Because I never told him, he never knew how I felt at the time and this was really hurtful for me. I just wanted him to ask me to go with him, but it never happen.

Laszlo's work was mainly on houses doing ducted heating and air-conditioning, depending on the season. When people wanted heating, he would have to crawl under houses and into other tight spots to complete the job. He would often come home muddy and cold and very tired. When they wanted air-conditioning in the summer he would have to crawl into the roof, which could often be as hot as 60C°. The tools were sometimes too hot to touch. It wasn't easy work and he had to account for every minute of his time, which could be difficult too. However he really needed the job, he didn't know where else he could go and was still struggling with the language, so he had to stick it out. It was a big stress on him because he felt responsible for the whole family.

One day I was at home and Csilla was home sick from school. She was asleep in her room when there was a knock on the door. It was Laszlo's boss. I was very surprised, because he hadn't really called around to our house before without Laszlo or his wife with him. I invited him in and we had coffee together and a bit of a chat. Then he said something and I really wasn't sure that I had understood him correctly, so I asked him again. He replied that he couldn't live without me. I was shocked – I had heard him correctly! I asked him what he was talking about and he said that he really wanted to be with me. I still wasn't really sure what he meant; I just couldn't believe that he had said that to me. I explained to him that I wasn't that kind of person and that I really loved Laszlo. I would never consider doing anything like that. He said that we didn't have to tell Laszlo. I said that I couldn't believe what I was hearing and couldn't understand how he could contemplate doing something like that. I then asked him to leave. He didn't want to go at first, he kept saying that nobody had to know and that he really needed me and wanted me. I was still in a state of shock and just told him to get out. I think I was very lucky that Csilla was at home; otherwise I don't know what would have happened. He finally left and I just sat down with my head spinning. I didn't know what to do. If I told Laszlo he would leave his job and we really needed that money, so I decided that I wouldn't tell him. Afterwards I made sure that I always avoided him wherever possible. If we were to go out and he was there, I made sure I never sat near him or had any contact with him. Luckily Laszlo hadn't noticed.

Chapter Eight

In the late 1980s the house prices in Melbourne were going up and up and we were starting to seriously consider buying a house. We decided that we would sell the jewellery to enable us to get some more cash together for a house deposit. Laszlo's boss's wife was Australian and a very nice lady and she offered to come with me to try and sell the jewellery. We went around to a few jewellery shops in the city to see what they would offer us. One shop had good gold prices but not for gold jewellery. We had thought that gold was gold wherever we went, but it didn't work like that. Only solid gold held its value, not gold jewellery. Nobody had told us that and we realised we would have been better off just bringing all the cash with us, but it was too late to worry about that now. Even though it was beautiful jewellery, they didn't pay for a particular style or particular work. We found out that while it was worth about $10,000 or $12,000 to buy, the maximum that we could squeeze out of anybody was $4,000. I told Laszlo and while we were disappointed that we wouldn't get the real value, we didn't need the jewellery and we did need the cash. So we took it back to that jeweller and got the $4,000. Afterwards a few people had suggestions, like putting it in the trading post, but it was too late then and we couldn't do anything about it. We hadn't gotten good advice to sell it through the jeweller, but we just had to accept things as they were.

We started to look for a house to buy. We went through heaps and heaps of display homes and I gathered many different brochures about the different designs and worked out which one would suit us best. We knew that we had the 5% deposit and most of the banks were offering a 95% loan, so we weren't too concerned. By this stage Laszlo was technically self-employed. The man he was working for had said to him that it was best if they formed a company. We paid $700 to purchase a company and Laszlo was then basically working as a sub-contractor. When we looked for houses we didn't really find anything at first, but we did notice that house prices were going up rapidly. Interest rates were about 17% back then and the price of houses were going up by almost $1,000 per week. We were starting to get worried as we couldn't save money fast enough to meet the increasing deposit amount. Eventually however we ended up looking in Endeavour Hills, which was a nice suburb that had a lot of new houses being built. We found one there that was $85,000 for the house and land, which was about 10 weeks away from completion. It was on a sloping block, so the house was built up, meaning there was room underneath as well. Also when you looked out the living room window, all the other houses in the neighbourhood were below, giving us a nice view. We talked to the builder and the agent and everything seemed to be fine. We had enough for a deposit and there weren't any other problems. After we signed the papers on a Thursday there was a three day cooling off period. We went home feeling very happy and excited about the prospect of owning our own home.

On Friday afternoon when Laszlo came home from work he looked really disappointed and told me that we had to knock back the house. His boss had told him that he didn't have a job for him anymore; that he wasn't getting much work and couldn't keep Laszlo on. We were really disappointed and very worried and couldn't work out what to do. On Sunday afternoon the builder called us and asked us what kind of brickwork we would like on the house and what kind of tiles. We were supposed to go and choose the tiles on the Monday. Because we had the three days cooling off period we were able to cancel everything without any penalty, but we hated to have to do it. The builder was pretty disappointed as well, but there wasn't really anything that either of us could do.

On Monday morning Laszlo's boss called and wondered why he hadn't come into work. Laszlo replied that he had told him that he didn't have a job anymore. His boss, however said that he had since had something come in and there was plenty of work for him to do. For some reason this man had told Laszlo a lie and because of it we had lost the house that we wanted. It was a bitter disappointment and we didn't look for houses for a while after that.

We eventually started looking again because Laszlo was really keen to get our own house. I called around to all the agents and explained that we were looking for something under $100,000. -. They basically all laughed and said that you couldn't get enithing for $100,000. - any more, so we had to go quite far away from the city to get a more affordable house. About an hours drive out from the city we saw some advertising for house and land packages for about $75,000. - to $80,000. - and decided to have a look around. It was a nice block that was close to the park and the area was already built in, which we liked. I hated the look of new building estates where every tree was cut down and all you can see were roof tops. There were two blocks left, so we decided that we would buy there. We signed the papers, because it seemed like a very good deal. We went to the bank first and asked Cecilia to come with us as her English was much better than ours. We were banking with the Commonwealth Bank and after we explained that we wanted a loan, they looked at our balances and said that they would need to see our business papers. The problem was that it was only a business in name and was to make the other man's paperwork easier. Laszlo was still actually working for weekly wages from his boss. After they looked through the papers they refused the loan, they didn't really explain why, they just said it had been declined. We didn't know at that time that if you were self-employed, it was much harder to get a loan. We were disappointed but didn't want to give up and went to another bank. After the 30 days was up and the deposit was due, the other bank refused our loan as well. This put us in a really bad situation and Laszlo's boss suggested that we go and see this particular Hungarian solicitor in the city. He was able to secure us a loan with a lending company.

Every weekend we would go down and have a look at the house site and take pictures, but we realised nothing was happening. We hadn't heard from the solicitor or from the builder and didn't know what was going on. We decided to call the solicitor. He said that he had forgotten to tell us that the builder had informed him that we would need much stronger foundations than first thought, which would cost an extra $2,000. -. If we paid this $2,000. - straight away then they could start building our house. We were very surprised that the soil test hadn't been done earlier but realised if we didn't pay this money then the house would never get started. We had to wait for a month or two to get the money together and they slowly started to build the house. At that time, we didn't know that when you purchase a house and land package, you don't have to start making the mortgage repayments until the house is finished. Because our solicitor had organised the whole thing, we had already starting making the mortgage repayments, even before the house was started.

It took them 11 months to build an 11 square house, which we found hard to believe. The neighbours had started their house after us and were living in theirs long before ours was completed. Even when it was finished the builder didn't want to give us the keys because there was an extra $2,000. - to pay. We had told them to leave the electrical work because Laszlo could do it, but somebody else had done it already, so there was that extra cost. He wouldn't give us the keys until the extra money had been paid.

Finally the house was built and everything was ready. We wondered though if the solicitor was actually helping us or if he was helping the builder instead. Every time we had a problem or complained to him about something he always said that it was best not to complain, because the builder could just walk out and leave the house half finished. We were forced to bite our tongues and not say anything and always had to come up with the extra money when it was requested. Looking back on it now, it was a bad experience and very stressful. We were so excited when we finally got the keys and could move in. Laszlo had bought a little trolley for $35. - so we could lift up the fridge and the washing machine. When we arrived at the house we found that they hadn't cleaned up outside at all. There were still bricks and other building materials lying around and inside the living room there were two extra sheets of plaster that had been left there, which we had to carry out. We didn't have carpets at that stage, we just had a concrete floor. In the 11 months that we had been waiting I had finished sewing all the curtains by hand, because I didn't have a sewing machine. They looked really good when we put them up.

A couple of weeks after we moved into our house, I was doing the washing up one day when I noticed a little head appearing in front of the window. It would then disappear for a few seconds and then reappear again. This happened a few times and I wondered what was going on, so Laszlo went outside. It turned out that there were a few little kids out there in the park and one of them was particularly interested in what was going on inside our house. Laszlo said to them, "come on kids, follow me". The kids were scared because they didn't know what Laszlo was going to do to them, but they followed him anyway. He brought them into the house and showed them around. Then he introduced me and the kids. They were really interested and seemed to enjoy the tour, but they never looked through our windows again! It was quite cute really. We found all the people in the street to be very nice. They gave us some plants as a welcome gift and were always offering us the use of a wheelbarrow or ladder, because they knew we didn't have anything like that yet.

We soon settled into our new house. One day I took the kids to school and I was driving home when I passed Laszlo. We had previously bought a second car for me to use. The Hungarian man had come with us and had arranged quite a good deal, but it was a hire purchase with a really high interest rate of about 29%. We decided that we wouldn't go ahead with it and didn't sign any papers. Then they tried to tell us that we owed them $500 because the registration had been transferred to my name. First of all we checked with the transport department and found out that it was definitely not registered in my name. We called the dealer and told them that the car was not registered in my name and that we definitely weren't going to pay the $500. We also questioned why they would have transferred the registration anyway when we hadn't signed any papers. It was pretty obvious that they took an opportunity to try and rip us off and considered us to be stupid idiots just because we couldn't speak English. The same man came and helped us out again looking for another car. We still had the 29% hire purchase agreement, but we got a much better deal this time and we were very happy with the car.

When Laszlo saw me he stopped the car and came over. I could see that he was very upset. He was shaking and could hardly talk. I asked him "What had happened?" I thought that it must have been bad news from back home, that somebody in his family must have died or something. He said that it wasn't anything like that but he was still too shaken to talk and had to go home and lie down. He went home and when I arrived, he could still hardly talk. He said that he needed to get his thoughts together, so I left him lying down for a while until he had calmed down. I was still very concerned though; I had no idea what could have made him so upset. Soon afterwards he came out and told me what had happened. His boss had accused him of stealing from worksites. He claimed that the only reason we could afford to build our home was because Laszlo had stolen fittings from new houses. Apparently this did happen sometimes. Thieves would come into an unfinished house and remove the carpet or the stove and because the builder was insured he could get another one. His boss said that was how we had managed to get our house, including the carpet. It was obvious that he had never been inside our house because we didn't have any carpet! Laszlo just said to him that he never wanted to see him or work for him ever again. His boss had also seen the little trolley that Laszlo had bought and had borrowed it. He liked it so much he then asked if Laszlo would sell it to him. Laszlo said OK, as he didn't really need it anymore, and the sale took place. His boss then asked for a receipt, so we gave him the receipt that we had received when we bought the trolley. At the time we bought it we didn't realise that the trolley wasn't printed on the receipt, something else was printed instead. When he noticed this, Laszlo's boss said that we were trying to rip him off and make extra money out of him. He said that we had probably stolen the trolley too and were lying about where we had bought it.

So here we were in a brand new house without carpet, we had a mortgage at 17.5% and two cars. One was paid for but the other had the hire purchase agreement with 29% interest. It was a very bleak situation to be in and we weren't sure what we would do. After the big shock of Laszlo losing his job, we panicked for a while but then realised that we would have to sit down and decide what to do next. We had never been on the dole before and as much as we didn't want to be, I said to Laszlo that we really didn't have a choice. Eventually he accepted that he would have to go and register with Social Security so we could at least have some money coming in. Laszlo was a very proud man and was embarrassed about the idea of queuing to ask for money from the government, but as I reminded him of the fact that we had two little girls to look after and that we needed to eat, he applied for the dole. Of course we would continue looking for work in the meantime, but the mortgage and car payments had to be made and there just didn't seem to be any other option. Eventually Laszlo got up the courage to go to the Social Security Office, but he soon ran into a big problem. They explained that he would need a separation certificate from his old boss before he could register for benefits. This was so he could prove that he was no longer working. When Laszlo came home he said that there was no way on Earth that he would go back to his boss to ask for anything. Even though we were in a desperate situation with no income and so many bills to pay, nothing would make Laszlo go back and talk to that man ever again. Looking back it seemed like maybe it was too strong a stand to take, but at the time that was the decision that was made.

We came back to the question of what we could possibly do to survive without any money coming in. We kept asking ourselves what we should do and in the beginning there didn't seem to be any real answers. Finally Laszlo came up with the idea that maybe we could fix up the little yellow Toyota and sell that. It still worked perfectly well, but it had sustained some minor damage such as dents and scratches in the paintwork. It was nothing major, but it would take some time and patience to fix up properly. Unfortunately we didn't have a shed at this house; in fact we didn't even have a fence at that stage because we just couldn't afford it. It was a bit of a problem because we didn't really have a place to store the tools and other things like that. We just had to stack them under the verandah or at the back of the house and hope that they didn't get wet or nobody stole them, so fixing up the car wasn't the easiest thing to do, but Laszlo soon got to work on it and put a lot of effort into making it worth selling. I just had to do the best I could with very limited things in the pantry, I think that I came up with some very interesting meals at that time. As the fridge and the pantry gradually emptied I just couldn't afford to replace a lot of the things because we were almost out of money. It was a very worrying situation to be in, but I did manage to be very creative.

Eventually Laszlo finished fixing up the car. It looked much better; the only problem was that the paint he got to fix up the scratches was a different shade of yellow from the rest of the car. So it looked a bit patchy in places! But it was clean and in perfect working order, so it was definitely in good enough condition to sell. We advertised it in the Trading Post and about one and a half weeks later a woman rang who was interested in buying it. She came to have a look and was very impressed; she didn't even mind the patchy paintwork. We asked for

$4,000 and she paid it without question. We did all the paperwork and finally we actually had a bit of cash in our hands again. It was such a relief, although we knew that we would have to be very careful with it. The first thing that we did was to pay our monthly bills, as most of them were overdue.

It was getting close to Christmas and once again we had a dilemma about what we could do and how much money we could spend. We had a lot of Hungarian friends and they were all very helpful in looking out for people who might want air-conditioning done. It turned out that some Hungarian people who had a small jewellery factory needed some air-conditioning installed and they asked Laszlo to come and have a look at it. He gave them a quote and they accepted it because they knew just how bad our financial situation was. They were happy to help out in that way. They were also very helpful in paying some money upfront for the unit and the other materials. This made a big difference to us and we really appreciated it. Laszlo found a suitable unit for them, but we had to go and pick it up from the other side of Melbourne. We had to take my car and borrow a trailer. This unit was so heavy though, that we had to drive in second gear the whole way (even though my car was automatic). It was a long, slow drive across the city – it took about two hours, but this job was very important to us. After Laszlo started work on the installation, one day he asked me if I would go and help him as he couldn't afford to pay anybody else. I agreed and went over to the factory with him. It was a very tall building and because the next buildings fence was so close, when Laszlo set the ladder up it was almost vertical. He didn't find it very scary to climb up there but I did and I ended up staying up on the roof all day, I didn't even need to go to the toilet. I had decided that there was no way I was going up and down that ladder more than once that day, even though I didn't need to be up there all the time. The people from the factory were very impressed that I was willing to spend the day helping Laszlo to get their job done. Eventually he was finished and they were very happy with the work that he had done. It was great to get the money for the job and to know that we were OK for a while, even though we still had real financial problems to worry about. Christmas was getting closer and it wasn't a nice time of year to have no money. The girls were really good about it, they understood what was going on and didn't expect us to give them things that we couldn't afford. However we still really wanted to give them something and to make it feel like a real Christmas, even though things weren't that good. Having grown up in Europe we did miss the traditional white Christmas and not having any presents made it seem even worse. We decided to make the best of things though. We had each other and we were all healthy, so there were worse things that could have happened to us.

I went to the nursery and bought a little live Christmas tree in a pot, which we then decorated to make things more festive. I had managed to buy quite a few little things for the girls, so at least they would get something on the day. Laszlo and I decided that we wouldn't get each other anything but we did want the girls to have some Christmas cheer. We decided to go to the beach for the day and to just enjoy ourselves, even though we didn't have a lot. We did have a nice day and an enjoyable lunch and when we got home, we surprised the girls by showing them their presents under the tree. The surprise on their faces was wonderful to see, they hadn't really been expecting anything and it was so nice that they didn't have to miss out completely. When the girls had finished opening all their presents I noticed another little jewellery box under the tree. I asked Laszlo what it was and he said that it was for me. I couldn't believe it and I said to him, "I can't believe that you got me some jewellery! We said we weren't getting presents for each other and now I feel really embarrassed because I don't have anything for you."

Laszlo replied that it wasn't from him it was from the man who owned the jewellery factory. He had been very happy with the work that Laszlo had done for him and was also very impressed that I had gotten up on the roof to help him out all day. So he gave it to Laszlo to give to me. It was a lovely necklace and matching bracelet and I was really touched that he had thought of me in that way. It made Christmas a bit brighter for all of us.

Our first Christmas in our own home wasn't quite what we had hoped it might be, but we had made the very best of a bad situation and with the support of family and friends it had turned out not too badly in the end.

It was very frustrating to have so little money when we wanted to do so much with our new house. We were comfortable enough but there were lots of little things that we just couldn't afford. It would have been nice to get some carpet, a shed for the tools or even to fix the garden up a bit, but we had to make the best of our situation until things started looking up again. We managed somehow, even when things seemed like they couldn't get any worse. Soon the holidays were over and the girls were back at school. Laszlo and I were both looking for jobs and we were prepared to do almost anything to earn some money. Finally Laszlo got an interview with an Australian man who was looking for somebody to help him with domestic air-conditioning installations. It was a bit of a drive, but we didn't really care – the job was much more important. Fortunately the man was very friendly and he and Laszlo got along really well right from the moment they met. He was happy to employ him and we were just so relieved that we had regular money coming in again. Not too long afterwards I also managed to find myself a job in the suburb that we used to live in. It was six hours a day in the kitchen of a hostel that cared for intellectually disabled people. Even though it was a long way away and we only had one car, I accepted the job because we desperately needed money. Laszlo had to start work at seven o'clock and I started at eight. Each morning he would load his tools into my car and I would drive him to his work, where he would have to unload his tools. He would then have to wait for his boss with his tools stacked around him! Fortunately it was about halfway to my job, so after I dropped him off I could continue on to my work. After finishing work for the day I would drive back home and when it was time for Laszlo to finish I would drive out to pick him up from wherever he had been working that day. We did this five days a week for four months and it was really hard and quite stressful. After four months we had kept up with all the mortgage and car payments and had managed to put aside about $1,000. -. We decided that we would put this towards a van for Laszlo, because it was too hard to keep going on the way we had been. A van was the most practical thing for him, because it meant that he had somewhere secure to keep his tools and he could also carry air-conditioning units in the back if he needed to. We looked around and finally found a suitable vehicle for $12,000. -. We paid the $1,000. - deposit and unfortunately had to have a hire purchase agreement for the rest, because there was no other way that we could have afforded it. We now had the mortgage and two car loans at 29% interest. It was a difficult situation to be in, but at least we had jobs and could start getting back on our feet financially. Things were much better than they had been a few months earlier.

I continued working in my job for a while longer, but eventually decided that I would give it up. It was an interesting job, but you did have to have the right personality to cope with working there. Working in the kitchen I had to clean up after breakfast, morning tea and lunch. They were lovely people but it could be very messy work. The people in the hostel all seemed to really like me. They would often come into the kitchen and hug me and would often take me into their rooms and tell me secrets or show me their special things. I didn't mind this at all, but it was quite a hard job and some people would have found it very difficult to cope with. Even though we still needed money, it wasn't worth the one hour driving time each way in heavy traffic to only work for six hours. A big chunk of the money I was earning was going towards petrol as well, so I resigned from there and started looking for another job a bit closer to home. I didn't really want to go back to cleaning houses, but I was prepared to try anything to bring in some extra money. I started looking around but there didn't seem to be much available in the paper. Eventually I just started going around to all the places I could think of like factories and shops and filling in an application form. Even after that I didn't hear anything back from any of these places, so I started looking a bit further away. It was then that I came across a mushroom farm. I had never worked on a farm before and didn't know what kind of work it was, but I filled in an application anyway. I also went to the nearby biscuit factory. Once again however, time went on and I didn't hear anything, which was disappointing. Then one day out of the blue I got a phone call from the mushroom farm asking me if I would like to go in for an interview. During the interview they explained how the mushrooms were grown and picked and what kind of work it would be. They also asked me if I had a fear of heights, because part of the job involved standing up on a platform that was about three metres high and didn't have any handrails. I told them that I didn't think I did, I had never really thought about it before. The interview seemed to go well and I was so happy when they rang back a few days later and offered me a job there. It would be wonderful to have some extra money coming in again.

I started work there on a Friday and after working for about five or six hours I came home with really bad pain! I could hardly move because my back was so sore. I thought to myself 'I can't do this', but at the same time I knew that I had to because we really needed that money. The mushrooms were grown inside a huge shed. The temperature was controlled at about 18 or 19C°. There were about five long shelves and each of these were five levels high. Some girls were picking on the floor on their hands and knees, then at the next level you could pick standing up. After that there was a platform with wheels that you had to climb up onto. It was really quite dangerous and scary too, because there weren't any handrails and if somebody accidentally bumped you, it wouldn't be hard to fall off. The mushroom boxes were on the shelf with you, so you had to be careful about that too. I did eventually get used to it and the girls that I worked with were really nice. We were all pretty careful and looked out for each other, as everybody had a turn up on the platform at some time or another.

Chapter Nine

One day Laszlo was at home by himself when he got a phone call from my brother. I couldn't believe it when he told me. Although the girls had been seeing each other for a couple of years, we hadn't actually spoken to my brother and his wife for about three years. It turned out that one of his friends wanted some heating installed in his house and he had heard through the Hungarian network that Laszlo did ducted heating installation. Laszlo accepted this job and went to see my brother. He ended up going inside their house and having a talk, mainly about the business. He then invite us all over to their house. We were a bit sceptical but decided that we would go. We had quite a nice time and then invited my brother's family back to our place. Even though we never actually said as much, the decision seemed to be made that we would not speak about the past and all the unpleasant things that had happened. We did however talk about things that had happened since arriving in Australia. My brother and his family were renting at first as well, but had since bought their own house. It was quite an old house that needed lots of renovating. In the beginning they basically had to live in one room, while they fixed up the rest of the house. It was obviously difficult for them in at first but they worked hard and things soon got better. Both of them had found jobs with Stegbar. My brother worked cutting glass and his wife assembled Venetian Blinds. It was very convenient for them to be working in the same factory because it was close to their home and they could travel together. This meant that they only needed one car. They were both earning good money and were able to save a lot. This allowed them to fix up their little house very nicely. The girls had also grown up a lot, even though we had been seeing them quite regularly. Now that things were so much better between us, we started seeing each other almost every weekend. We would often go to the markets together, or just visit each other's houses. If we had a birthday in the family we would celebrate that together as well. I was happy that we had made amends. Although the things that had happened in Hungary and Austria had hurt us a lot, I didn't want to hold a grudge against my only brother. It felt good to have some family living in the same city when the rest of our relatives were on the other side of the world.

Things settled down now that we had more money coming in. Laszlo continued to work at his job and the girls were doing really well at school, which was wonderful to see. Csilla was really clever on the monkey bars, she was always hanging off them and sometimes I would have a heart attack just watching her. One day she asked me if she could do gymnastics lessons, as one of her friends was doing it. We went along to the club and she had a try out. They said she could join and told us the training schedule. She started taking gymnastics lessons once a week. She really enjoyed it and the coach was impressed with her skills. She was often involved in different competitions and all the parents would take turns driving the kids all over Melbourne. We were really proud of her and what she could do. Anita was also a wonderful daughter; she studied really hard and did so well at school. The girls were really good to each other. They got along so well and always helped each other out.

As time went by we decided that we needed a study at home for business related matters, but we couldn't afford to extend the house. We decided to move the girls into the master bedroom to give them more space, then we took the second largest room and converted the third bedroom (which was really tiny) into a study. Laszlo then made the girls some specially designed bunk beds, which had shelves and a desk each underneath. This gave them plenty of space and they were very happy and comfortable sharing that room.

Before too long it was almost Christmas again. We would never forget just how bad things had been the year before, but it was also good to see how much we had accomplished since then. Money was still very tight, but we were much more on top of things and our life had settled down once again. Around this time we had some news from home. My Dad had decided that he would like to come and visit us. He planned to buy his own ticket but wanted to work with Laszlo while he was here, so that he could earn enough to replace the cost of the ticket and also maybe buy some other things for himself while he was here. The problem was that Laszlo didn't have a lot of work himself at that time. Things were a bit slow and our mortgage and car repayments were taking almost all of our money anyway. I talked to my Dad and asked him to consider coming at another time, when things were a bit better for us. I knew that we wouldn't be able to afford to buy him beer and cigarettes and my Dad liked both those things. Also when you have a relative visiting, especially a parent, you really want them to have a great time. To do that you have to be able to show them around and take them lots of places and I knew that just wouldn't be possible if he came at that time. As much as I wanted to see Dad again, if he was coming to the other side of the world I wanted him to really enjoy it. I did my best to convince him but he wouldn't listen and booked his ticket to come at the end of December. We picked him up on the 28th of December, so the first big change for him was the weather. He had come out of a freezing European winter to a hot Australian summer, which took some adjustment. He did manage quite well though. While Dad had a really good time during his stay with us, I knew that he wanted a bit more than we could afford to give him. After he had been there a few days he asked for some beer and said that he would like some cigarettes. We only drank juice at home, but Dad didn't think that it was the kind of thing that men drank. I really wanted to give Dad those things and I felt bad that I couldn't, but food and petrol were our main priorities and we just couldn't afford any luxuries. Dad also got a bit upset when he wanted to help us out around the house a bit, but didn't have any tools to do so. I explained to him that Laszlo took all his tools with him in the van to work each day. As Laszlo was the only one who used the tools we didn't need two sets. If he was at home then his tools were there too. On another occasion we had decided to put a little pool in the back yard. It was only a small, round one but it would be nice to cool off in on a hot summer day, so one weekend Dad and Laszlo dug a hole for the pool to go in (we were putting it half into the ground). It was a very hot day and in summer Melbourne has a lot of little flies that are attracted to sweat. Because they were working so hard, these flies were all over Laszlo and Dad. They almost drove Dad crazy. He would angrily shoo them away and sometimes he was almost hitting himself in the face because he was so mad. While it was nice of him to help us out, it made him quite aggravated as well. During the day whilst we were at work he would mainly stay at home and read, but he also enjoyed going down to the bus stop to get the girls after school. At night we talked a bit and most of the time things weren't too bad. He was happy enough, but I knew that he expected more from us.

My sister in law had never liked Dad, even when we were all still in Hungary. We didn't see very much of them at the time that Dad was visiting. It was very uncomfortable for all of us the few times that we went to visit them and my sister in law stopped my brother from coming over to our place. They were quite well off financially and could have afforded to give Dad things that we couldn't. They also went for a week's holiday to Sydney, but didn't tell us about it. This would have been a good opportunity for Dad to see some more of Australia and we were annoyed that they didn't mention they were going. They didn't want us to find out about it at all, but it's a small world and word got back to us. I thought it was very selfish of them because they knew how bad our financial situation was and they also knew how much Dad wanted to go and see other places while he was here. In the whole three months that Dad was visiting, they only invited him to their place for dinner once. He never went to stay with them at all. One thing that we did do with Dad while he was there was a visit to Phillip Island to watch the penguin parade. This was something that you would never, ever see in Hungary so we decided that we would definitely go there. Dad really enjoyed this outing, even though we didn't see many penguins. We had sat for hours in the freezing cold waiting for them to arrive. Finally at about 11pm two penguins came out of the water. They walked up, looked around a bit and seemed to think to themselves that it wasn't time yet and got back in the water again. We couldn't believe it! Then Dad said, "Well I've seen enough. The rest of them will probably just come out the same way". I almost wanted to strangle Dad then – we had been sitting there all those hours almost freezing our bums on the concrete steps and he decided that two was enough! It was just one of those situations where you had to laugh. As we walked up to the car, we saw quite a few penguins and Dad kept asking "How they got up there so fast?" I explained that they were actually different penguins than the ones we had seen earlier. We saw quite a few more penguins and he kept asking the same question each time. I finally said that if he asked me once again I would just leave him there! We did enjoy the day anyway and it was nice that Dad had a good time.

Throughout Dad's stay the conflict between him and my sister in law was always a problem. I'm not sure exactly what was said between them, but it was an ongoing difficulty to deal with. One particular night stands out in my memory. We were at home watching TV when the phone rang. I answered and found out that it was my niece. She was crying and very upset and told me that there had been a big argument at her place. Apparently my sister in law had said that she wanted to divorce my brother, there was yelling and screaming going on and the girls were really upset. She begged me to come over and help them. Laszlo and I didn't say anything to Dad, but we quickly got into the car and went over to their place. We tried to sort out what was happening. My sister in law was saying that she just couldn't stand our Dad that she didn't want him around at all and didn't want to have anything to do with him. My brother was saying that this was his father after all and he couldn't just ignore him. My sister in law said that she wanted a divorce because of our father.

To me this was a pretty silly argument because Dad was only here for a visit and he was staying with us anyway. This kind of thing had happened before and I decided that I had had enough. I didn't want to fight with my brother anymore but I couldn't deal with my sister in law. I actually took my brother's side this time. After that night I just had to ask my Dad nicely to go home. This was a really hard thing for me to do and I hated having to do it, but I couldn't cope with the conflict anymore. I didn't ever want to go back to the way things had been when I wasn't speaking to my brother and his family, so I had to do something to keep the peace. Finally we went into the city and booked his flight home for the end of March. When we took him to the airport, Dad hugged me goodbye and thanked me for all that we had done for him while he was there. He said that he had had a really good time and that he hoped he would see us again soon. It was really hard to say goodbye and I cried all the way home from the airport. I felt like I had kicked him out, even though I had only asked him to leave because things were so difficult. I felt bad that we hadn't been able to give him everything that he would have liked and that there had been conflict. It was a really difficult and emotional time for me and it still makes me sad to think about it now. I think that night changed me inside in some way. It made me see more clearly what I had and made me appreciate it more. I decided that my sister in law had manipulated the situation to get what she wanted, but I also decided that I wouldn't let her do that again. I would no longer interfere with their family life and I would not let a situation like the one with my father happen again. In any case things happen for a reason and I had learnt some important lessons from this experience. Soon afterwards I wrote my Dad a letter and apologised for what I had done. I explained how bad I felt and how hard it was not knowing when we would see each other again. With our financial situation there was no way we could afford a trip home again in the near future. I felt a bit better when I had done that but I never forgot about it and it would always make me feel a bit sad.

Time went on and life got back to normal again after Dad's visit. Csilla was getting really good at her gymnastics and was spending a lot more time training. She was really talented and we were so proud of what she could do, even though it did scare us when we saw some of the things she did on the beam or uneven bars. I was still working at the mushroom farm. I had soon gotten used to the work and my back didn't hurt any more, which was good. Laszlo's work was also going well. Sometimes he had a lot of work and other times not much at all, but we weren't doing too badly. Anita was at high school by this stage and was really starting to grow up. It was around this time that Laszlo's brother decided that he would like to come and live in Australia too. Since we had left Hungary things had changed a lot. The government had changed, the Russian soldiers had been removed and it was now a free country. That meant that you could come and go as you pleased and didn't have to escape anymore. If you had relatives anywhere in the world you were free to apply for residency there. We were able to sponsor them, but it was a very long and quite complicated process. There was a lot of paperwork on both sides and many other details to be sorted out. The whole procedure took almost two years. In order to sponsor them we had to be Australian citizens, so that was something else that we had decided to do. We wanted to become citizens anyway and this was a good reason to do so. Laszlo's brother and his family landed in December; a year after my Dad had arrived for his holiday. The young man next door decided to move home and put his house up for rent. This was a really lucky break for us as we managed to get it for Laszlo's brother's family. It meant that they arrived to a furnished house, which was a real advantage. Having us so close by was also a big help for when they were settling in and we were happy to be able to help them so much.

Chapter Ten

The same December that Laszlo's brother arrived we had an opportunity to go on a holiday to the Gold Coast. We were really looking forward to it because we hadn't been on a holiday since we arrived in Australia. We couldn't believe that it would only cost $300 per week on the Gold Coast at Christmas time, as this was the peak holiday season. Another

Hungarian family had been to the same place every year for eight years. The owner of the complex knew them very well and said that if they bought family and friends they could get a discount. There were originally three Hungarian families who were supposed to be going, but one of them couldn't make it, so we asked Laszlo's brother if they would like to come up with us and they agreed. They had some money and could afford to pay, so it was a nice opportunity for them. They had only arrived on the 10th of December and by the 20th were going on a holiday to the Gold Coast. It was a happy arrival in Australia for them! We went in Laszlo's work van. It was really only a six-seater car but Csilla and our niece were both really small and could fit in quite easily. It wasn't exactly legal to have us all in there, but it was comfortable enough. About 200km from Melbourne we had to stop because my niece was really sick. Her mother then told us that she forgot to mention that she gets carsick! Fortunately she soon recovered and after a while she got used to the motion of the car.

The kids played together and the adults talked, so that helped to pass the time. We also stopped quite often so that also helped to make the journey less monotonous. At one of the places we stopped for petrol, we decided to get something to eat, as we were all hungry, however as soon as we removed the wrapper from the sandwiches that we bought the bread was immediately covered in little black flies! We eventually worked out a system to stop the flies settling on our lunch. We all walked around the van in circles, which didn't give the flies a chance to settle on the sandwiches. We felt a bit silly doing it but it was the only thing that worked. It was really quite funny to watch us. When we finished eating we decided that we were leaving as fast as possible to escape the flies, however when we got into the van we realised that it was now full of those tiny little flies as well! As we drove off we had to open all the windows to get rid of them. Fortunately after a few kilometres they were all gone and we could close the windows again. On our first day we covered about 1100 kilometres. We had all swapped seats during the day, as the front was the most comfortable position and it was only fair to let everybody have a turn. Laszlo did all the driving, so he was very tired by the end of the day. We spent our first night in Moree. The other Hungarian couple that we were travelling with had gotten there ahead of us and had booked us a motel.

We had quite an interesting experience at Moree. The sky was pitch black and we were looking at the stars when we saw a little tiny flashing light that was zooming all around the sky. It definitely couldn't have been a plane or a shooting star, so we thought that it might have been a UFO. We watched it zigzag around the sky for quite a while but we still weren't sure exactly what it was.

We got up at five o'clock the next morning so we could get an early start for the rest of our trip. It was still dark and it was a bit cold when we set off. We left the motel with the other Hungarian couple and decided that we would follow them the rest of the way. They had warned us to be careful, as they always seemed to hit a kangaroo on their way to Queensland. They told us how they could jump out in front of the car without warning. Sure enough we hadn't gone very far out of Moree when we heard a big bang and saw that this other man had hit a kangaroo. It was very sad to see this poor kangaroo die. I love all animals and it wasn't very nice to see one dying like that.

We kept driving on for a while and just as the sun was rising, our friends in front of us started slowing down as they were having car trouble. Apparently when they hit the kangaroo it did some damage to the car. We both stopped for a while and our friend had a look at the car to see what was wrong. I was amazed to see him go to the back of his car and take out a pair of white cotton gloves. He explained that he didn't want to get grease on his hands while he fixed the car. It just seemed quite funny to see somebody fixing a car wearing white gloves! He actually worked in a biscuit factory so he had dozens of pairs of these gloves and he could use them and throw them away when he needed to. He managed to fix the car and we were soon on our way again. It was around lunchtime when we got to the Queensland border. It was really beautiful going through the Great Diving Range; I was just amazed at the landscape that we drove past. We were also amazed at some of the little fruit and vegetable stalls at some of the little villages that we passed. They just left the fruit and vegetables out beside the road and had an honesty box to put the money in. There wasn't anybody to check and everybody always paid. In fact if people didn't have the correct money they would put extra in the box, rather than less. Coming from Hungary where there wasn't that kind of trust, it was a really amazing thing to see. If you had done that there people would steal the whole stall, not to mention the fruit and the money!

Soon after crossing the border we arrived at the place we were staying. It was a really nice little hotel that was close to the ocean and the river. We had a unit on the first level and the other Hungarian couple were next to us. Laszlo's brother and his family were on the ground level. Just outside their unit was the pool, which was great for them. As soon as we put our things inside and settled in a bit we all jumped into the pool to cool off. We were enjoying the beautiful weather and also just being on holidays and relaxing. Being at the Gold Coast at Christmas time was a really fun experience as there was so much happening. We loved the beach. The ocean particularly amazed Laszlo's brother's family because they had just arrived from Hungary, which of course has no oceans. Seeing all this beautiful surf and white sand was a particularly welcoming experience for them. We went all around the Gold Coast and saw all the sights that we had heard about. We went to Brisbane for a day but it was extremely hot. Unlike the Gold Coast, which had the nice little ocean breeze, the buildings in the city made it feel much hotter. We went to the Myer Centre and had an enjoyable time, particularly the kids. We also went to Byron Bay for one day and had a really good time. We went to the lighthouse at the most Eastern point of Australia and took some photos. The scenery was just beautiful. We went to one of the National Parks that was inland and once again the scenery was just breathtaking. There was a gorgeous waterfall, which was nice to cool off in as it was a hot day. Just before we left Anita came to me and said that she thought she was getting her first period. I was thinking to myself 'oh great' because we were in the middle of nowhere and there were no shops or anything nearby. We didn't know what to do and then our Hungarian friends remembered their supply of white gloves. Poor Anita had to improvise with these gloves but they were OK for a temporary measure. It was good to get back to the shops though to get the proper products.

We had a really wonderful holiday but I did get a little bit cranky sometimes because when you are the woman you still have to organise meals and shopping. Even when you are enjoying yourself on holidays you still have to eat. We couldn't afford to eat out all the time so I still had to make the meals, even if they were simpler ones than you would have at home. Not having to get up and go to work was just wonderful but getting the meals ready was kind of like being at home sometimes. Laszlo and the kids would always be in the pool or at the beach so for them it was a real holiday away from everything. I did complain about it a bit, but because we couldn't afford to eat out there wasn't much that I could do about it. I understood that we couldn't afford it but I would have liked it if he could have helped me out a bit sometimes so I could get more of a break too. At one stage the van actually broke down and we had to take it to a mechanic to get fixed. We were a bit concerned and were worried about what might happen on the way back. It was fine however, and we didn't have any more problems.

Both of the girls could swim so they had a lot of fun in the water. My niece couldn't swim though, but she still wanted to do what the other girls were doing. This caused a few problems sometimes because she would scream a lot when she was in the water. She was quite different to both of our girls and I guess we kind of realised that their family was quite different to ours, even though they were brothers. However that was something that we had to get used to, now that they had come to live in Australia as well.

We were really taken with the wonderful weather up in Queensland. One morning as we enjoyed the sun on the terrace at our holiday unit we discussed how we could definitely handle living up in Queensland permanently. We thought the climate and the lifestyle was so good that we really began to consider moving up indefinitely. We decided that we would probably like to be somewhere near the Gold Coast, but first we had to go back to Melbourne and settle back into life there for a while.

On the way home we went on the Pacific Highway for a change of scenery. We stopped in Sydney so we could have a look around. We visited the Opera House and just walked around the city. We found a motel somewhere in Liverpool to stay. It wasn't a very nice area but it wasn't too expensive and we could put up with it for just one night. We then left Sydney and soon arrived back home in Melbourne. In some ways it was nice to be home again but the letterbox was just full of bills, which was quite depressing. It was hard to get back to reality and think about going back to work again after having such a wonderful holiday.

After we arrived back from our holiday and things settled down again I helped Laszlo's brother and his family enrol in the language school and organised all their Medicare cards and bank accounts. Because I had been through it all myself, I could offer them a lot of practical help. I could also translate for them when they were getting their licence and other day-to-day things. They soon settled in reasonably well, although they did have some language problems. They didn't speak a word of English so the language school was a real necessity and a big help for them too. They had a little girl and a son who was 16. It was very hard for him because he was a teenager and had to start all over again in a whole new country. School was very difficult as he couldn't speak any English and he didn't know anybody. For my niece it was easier because of her age. She went to the same school that Csilla was at, so having a familiar face there made it much easier for her. I took the girls to school each morning and picked them up which also made an easier transition. Being younger she picked up the language much faster.

The girls had quite a few friends at school and they would sometimes invite them over for dinner. These friends were always worried at first what the Hungarians would be eating. I could see the looks on their faces, they just seemed to be thinking that the food would be strange or something! They were polite enough not to say anything, but I could tell they were worried. They were always relieved when they tasted the food and found that they liked it. It was usually nothing special, just some dishes that we would normally have. All of the girls' friends enjoyed my cooking and would compliment me on how nice it was. I know they were all surprised that they liked it, but they always made sure they told me how much they enjoyed eating at our house.

We both continued to work hard at our jobs so we could pay all our bills, but we never seemed to get on top of things. We were behind with our mortgage payments and we didn't like being in that situation. We also didn't have knowledge of some of the rules that we were supposed to follow. For example we didn't know that even though Laszlo had his own business that we were supposed to write out wages each week – we would just use his earnings for food or bills as we needed to. This would prove to be a problem with an accountant later on. We just didn't know at the time that we were supposed to do things any differently.

Having Laszlo's brother close by was good for a while but we did have some problems too. My niece always used to come over every afternoon and my girls got a bit tired of that after a while. When I was growing up, we always had to worry about pleasing the neighbours. If somebody came over to play and I didn't like them I was never allowed to send them home because my mother would say, "What will the neighbours think?" There were many times I had to play with kids that I didn't like just because my mother said so. When the girls started to get a bit annoyed I knew I would have to do something. The last straw came one day when my niece closed the car door on Csilla's leg. I went over to their house and sat down with them and explained what was going on. I suggested that she could perhaps have some of her own friends over to play and just come over to our house from time to time. I explained that the reason I was telling them this was so that the girls could still be friends and not end up hating each other because they spent too much time together. They were quite surprised to hear what I had to say – I understand that it's not nice to hear bad things about your own child – but I knew that I had to do it as it was making all of us unhappy. I told Laszlo what I had done when he came home and he was quite angry about it. He said I was only doing it because it was his brother and that the girls 'hated' her. I replied that they didn't hate her, it just wasn't healthy to spend so much time with each other. He thought I had offended his family. In any case a few weeks later they decided that it would be a good idea if they moved somewhere else and I thought that it was best for everybody if they did. They found a place that wasn't too far away and moved there. There wasn't any arguments or bad feelings, they understood my point of view and had decided to move of their own free will. After they had moved away we only saw them every few weeks or so, the girls got along much better and I knew that I had done the right thing by saying something.

One night a guy came around and offered us a good deal with life insurance. Back then we didn't really have a particularly good knowledge of Australian systems and rules, so we didn't always know what was a good deal and what was a bad one. We had thought, however that this sounded like a good arrangement. He explained that our contributions would be a percentage of Laszlo's wages and it would be superannuation and life insurance. Because Laszlo didn't have set wages, the figure we gave him was the company earning for each month. We paid this amount for almost a year before our accountant alerted us to the fact that we were paying too much. He explained that we couldn't afford to keep paying this amount. We had to cancel the whole policy and because we chose to cancel it we couldn't recover any of our contributions. We lost several thousand dollars and learnt a hard lesson. There was nothing we could do about it and we just had to accept the fact that the money was gone.

After this experience we started looking at ways we could simplify our debts. Our mortgage payments were high and so were our car payments. At that time the banks started letting you combine your debts together to make just one monthly payment that was usually lower than the others combined. We started trying to do that as it would save us a lot of money. We went to see a lot of banks and building societies but none of them could help us. They all looked through our payments and said that this particular system would not work for us. We really couldn't understand why it wouldn't but they all said the same thing. They said that if we put all our debts together then it would cost us even more per month in repayments. We really couldn't see why that would happen but they all said the same thing. We had to give up on the idea, even though we thought it would have worked really well for us.

We still saw my brother and his family regularly. It was sometimes once a month or a bit less often than that, but we were often socialising with them. Sometimes they would come to our house and sometimes we would go to theirs or we would go somewhere together. When it was my sister in law's birthday one year, we went around to see her and wished her a happy birthday. All of the family was there, including their older daughter's boyfriend. My brother was outside with the kids and my sister-in-law was inside. After we wished her a happy birthday and gave her the presents we went outside to see my brother. When we went out we noticed that the older daughter and her boyfriend were ignoring us. They didn't talk to us at all and pretended we weren't there. When we actually tried to speak to them and have a conversation they just turned their backs to us. We really didn't know what was going on. It was pretty obvious that something was wrong but we had no idea what it was. Eventually we went back inside and talked to my brother and his wife, but the conversation was just average, they didn't tell us what was wrong. They always seemed dissatisfied with their life. They didn't like their jobs, they thought that Australians were all stupid, that everything was too expensive and other things like that. It was quite annoying to listen to this all the time. They always concentrated on the negative things rather than positive. My sister in law had a brand new kitchen and she had the latest model of all the appliances. I didn't even have a microwave back then but I was happy to be in Australia living in our own little place and enjoying the lifestyle that we had. We both had jobs, even though we weren't earning very much, but we had done quite well for ourselves overall.

On the way home I asked Laszlo if he had noticed that something really weird was going on. He agreed that things had been quite strange and strained with my niece. When I got home decided to call my sister in law and ask her what was going on as I couldn't stand just wondering about it anymore. I asked her if something was wrong because my niece was ignoring us. She replied that yes there was something wrong. I then asked her if it involved us in some way and she said that it did. I asked her what it was all about because I wanted to know what I had done wrong! She then said that my niece did not ever want to speak to me again. She said when my father had been visiting he had said something to my brother that had caused an argument with my niece. After this argument my brother had kicked her out and she now had to live with her boyfriend. I listened to the story with a bit of surprise, as I hadn't noticed that she wasn't talking to her father. I then asked what any of that had to do with me. She replied that because I was the one who had invited my father out, the whole thing was my fault! I agreed that I had invited my father to stay but I pointed out that he wasn't just my father he was my brother's father too! She refused to listen to that, instead she said that her daughter blamed me and did not want to talk to me or have anything to do with me anymore. I really couldn't understand the logic behind this argument but I thought that if she wanted to be like that then that was her problem. An interesting thing was that she ended up marrying her boyfriend anyway and they have stayed together ever since. Perhaps she should have thanked my father for saying something to my brother - which made her live with her boyfriend - because they loved each other anyway! It was a really strange thing to have happened and it was quite sad that they wanted to be so petty about things. I have never spoken to my niece since and I guess that it hasn't really affected me that much. It was another bad situation with my brother and his family that I would rather not have happened. We still kept in touch but we never talked about the situation with my niece.

Chapter Eleven

Because our business was always up and down we began to think about maybe doing something different. We thought about it for a while but didn't come up with anything right away. Then one day we came a cross a caravan that my brother's next door neighbours had. It was very old and quite wrecked as the walls were all smashed in, but the basic structure was OK. We were thinking that maybe we could fix it up and use it as a food van at markets or sporting events. We thought that this was something that my sister in law and I could do to bring in some extra money. My brother asked the neighbours if we could have the caravan and they said we could. They didn't even want any money for it, they were just glad to see it go. We took it to our place because we had enough room on our block. The shell was perfect; it was just the walls and everything that needed rebuilding. It was a bit rusty but still structurally sound. We never got around to turning it into a food van, but it stayed in our backyard.

Even though I had my job at the mushroom farm I was still frustrated that I was not able to use my drafting skills. Then finally one day through our network of Hungarian friends I finally got an opportunity to do some drafting work again. I designed a house for some people – I drew the plan, I went to the council and got all the forms and other necessary paperwork and permits to build the house. As much as I had enjoyed doing drafting work again, I had decided that I was not going to leave the mushroom farm unless I could get full time drafting work. I didn't enjoy working there but that money put food on the table and allowed us to pay off our other debts. A few months after I designed that first house Laszlo was doing some work for a Vietnamese family group. They built houses and they had their own architect. Except for Laszlo, who did the domestic air-conditioning, all the other people who worked for them were Vietnamese. One day he mentioned that I was a draftsperson who could design family homes. One of the part owners then said that he would like to meet me and to see some of my drawings. I was so excited, I went over to his place and showed my portfolio and explained what experience I had. He said that he would employ me to design one house per week. They also paid per square metre as well, which was excellent money. It was much, much better than the mushroom farm! Finally I could go back to doing what I really loved. I was just over the moon, I was so happy and excited to be working as a draftsperson again. I was glad to go to the mushroom farm and tell them that I was quitting! The people that I had worked with there were nice but I was just so glad to be doing what I was trained for.

Every Monday they would give me a sketch and I would have until Friday to finish the drawing. It was up to me how fast or slow I did the work, so that gave me the opportunity to take Csilla to gymnastics as she would go there most afternoons after school. Sometimes she would stay as late as 8 o'clock. It was great to have such flexible working conditions and the pay was excellent. This went on for almost three months and I was just enjoying the work so much, as well as being able to make some extra payments on our debts. Then one Monday I got a drawing as usual but throughout the week things kept changing on the drawing, every time I got back to the office the next morning something was different. It wasn't my fault; the customer just wanted some changes. This meant that I couldn't finish the drawing within a week, it took me two weeks instead. I was only getting paid every second Friday instead of every Friday. This wasn't fair though, because I was still doing the same amount of work but because it was on the same drawing I was only getting paid for half my work. This went on for three weeks and then I stopped getting drawings. They said I could stop by the office to see if any customers came in wanting drawings, so for three weeks I was in the office and was often answering the phone when they were out. Or I was just sitting there doing nothing. But I wasn't getting any more drawings to do and I wasn't getting paid anything because our agreement only covered me doing drawings. After three weeks I just asked them what was going on and they said that it was slow and we would have to wait and see what was going to happen. I explained that I didn't want to leave there, that I loved drawing and appreciated the chance to work, but I also said that because I was there in the office that I should get paid some minimal amount if I was answering the phone and helping them out. They said that they couldn't afford that. I was really disappointed and actually ended up having a big argument with them. I don't know where I got the courage because normally I wouldn't have done something like that. I told them that it was unfair to me and that they owed me money for the last three weeks and that it wasn't right what they were doing. In the end I left and all the way home, which was a half an hour drive, I was crying because I was just so disappointed that this drafting job hadn't worked out after waiting for so long. Everything had been going along so well so I really don't know what happened and why they ended up treating me so badly.

After this drafting job was finished I felt really empty inside and I just didn't know what to do. I really didn't want to go back to the mushroom farm but I just didn't know where else to turn. I knew that I wouldn't be able to work anywhere else as a draftsperson because nobody would give me the chance to prove myself. I was thinking that I wasn't getting any younger and that there just didn't seem to be any options open to me. It was a really hard time. I went out looking for work again but I couldn't find anything, which was also very disappointing.

Around this time we were thinking about getting a dog. Back in Hungary we had a German Shepherd and we decided that we would like to get that kind of breed again. This time, however we wanted to get a male puppy. We looked through the papers and found a few good breeders. First of all however we had to make a gate so he wouldn't be able to escape, so one weekend Laszlo and I made a gate and the block was secure. We were then able to go and find a dog. We spoke to the breeder and then went to see him when the puppies were about eight weeks old. There were about five puppies; two females and three males. They were purebred, vaccinated and had papers. They were black, longhaired German Shepherds. They let them all out and they were running around on the grass. The biggest dog came towards us and we ended up choosing him. Laszlo said to me later that he was the one he was thinking about anyway and I had thought the same thing. We called our new dog Jack. Our other dog back in Hungary had been named Jack as well. He was just a beautiful little fluff ball and we were very happy that he was ours. We were a bit worried about taking him in the car, it wasn't that far but he was so young. I had a blanket with me that we put around him so I could hold him on my lap. He was fine for the trip home, he didn't cry or anything. The girls were so excited when we got home and couldn't wait to get him inside and play with him. We all thought he was the most gorgeous dog we had ever seen but he was extremely smelly! Because he had been with all the other dogs in the shed he really smelt quite bad, so we made him a little bed in the laundry and when it was time to go to bed we closed the door. He was quiet for a while but then he started crying. We didn't really know what to do so we let him cry a bit and after a while he settled down and went to sleep. The next day when Laszlo was at work and the girls were at school, he started following me everywhere around the house. Every time I turned around he was just behind my feet just like a little shadow. I really loved him right from the beginning so I didn't mind that he was following me. I couldn't stand the smell though and decided that I just had to wash him. I put him in the bath and he was fine, he didn't cry or anything while I washed him. After his bath he was so clean and he smelled fresh, so I wrapped him up in a towel and held him like a baby and he actually started to suck my finger. He eventually went to sleep with my finger in his mouth. He was just so cute like a little baby, I have never forgotten that moment.

We all loved Jack and he was instantly a part of our family. It was lucky that I was at home when we got him because he needed to be fed three or four times a day for the first three months and I could do that. I took him to the vet for his injections because back in Hungary we had two puppies that died from Parvo

Virus, so we wanted to make sure that Jack was protected. We didn't let any other dogs near him and really looked after him well. The first day I took him into the garden he was quite timid and would only go a little distance away and would then come back. Then each day he would go a bit further and get a bit braver. After a week or two he would run all around the yard and really enjoy himself. We had a big back yard so he had plenty of room to explore and play.

When Jack was about three months old we started to do obedience classes with him. We would take him every Sunday and he was a very clever dog. He was always the first in running but he was always a bit grumpy with the other dogs. They all knew not to come too close to Jack. There was another dog there called McGregor who was also a German Shepherd, but she was just huge compared to the other dogs. Everybody told us that Jack would be really big when he grew up because he had huge paws. After about six months or so we were busy for a few weeks and missed several obedience classes. When we went back we could really see how much Jack had grown. When he was close to McGregor he was much bigger than her. We were amazed that he could have grown so much in such a short time. We had always thought McGregor was so huge and now our dog was bigger. When he was with us every day we didn't notice the change but it was easy to see when you compared them after a few weeks.

Meanwhile Csilla continued to go really well with her gymnastics. She took part in many competitions and would always come home with lots of medals. Her coach was really proud of her and she just loved what she did. I was amazed watching her sometimes doing 200 sit-ups and 200 push-ups. She was really skinny and still quite tiny but she was also really strong. I couldn't believe some of the things that she could do on the beam. People were always amazed that somebody so small could be so strong and could do such difficult things. She ate all right but at one stage the coach told her that she had to be very careful about what she ate. He told her that she shouldn't eat any junk food and that to be a gymnast you had to be very slim. A few months later her teacher called me in and told me that she noticed that Csilla was not eating her lunch at school. She would eat a little bit of it and would throw the rest in the bin. I had no idea she was doing this because her lunchbox was always empty or there was just a little bit left. I really appreciated that her teacher had paid so much attention to what she was doing and that she had told me about it. I talked to Csilla and she admitted that she was putting most of her lunch in the bin each day. She said it was because the coach had told her that she had to stay skinny if she wanted to be a gymnast. Luckily Laszlo had done a lot of sports and he talked to her about it. He told her that if she wanted to be strong and have energy that she had to eat properly. He explained that because she was working so hard she was easily burning off all the calories that she was taking in. It was really hard for her to understand but we did catch this in time. It hadn't developed into something serious, which was very lucky. The thought that she could have developed anorexia or bulimia was very scary. It's easy to understand how this can happen with young girls. The coach can say something and young girls take it so seriously, even if it means their health will suffer. Girls of that age can be so easily influenced. Csilla was only about nine at that time, too young to have to worry about such things.

Both the girls also did well at school and had lots of friends. They would often have their friends around or would go to their houses. As Anita got older she was invited to sleepovers at her friends places. This was a new experience for us because in Hungary that wasn't a common thing to do. Laszlo didn't let Anita sleep over as he thought that everybody should go home at bedtime. Naturally enough Anita was quite devastated by this because she wanted to do what her friends were doing. I could understand how she felt but at that time I used to usually go along with what Laszlo decided, even if I didn't really agree with it. This did cause arguments of course, because being a teenager Anita was getting to the age where she often considered whatever she said was right and what we said was wrong. Anita was a stubborn girl anyway, so this also meant that we had a few disagreements. We knew, however that this was all part of being parents and they really were only quite minor problems. Overall both the girls were good daughters and we were very proud of both of them.

One day we got a phone call from Hungary from some friends of ours who wanted to come and settle in Australia. What they needed from us was a letter of invitation. Rather than applying for residency they had decided to come on a six months tourist visa and then apply for residency while they were here. They did have some friends or relatives in Sydney but I'm really not sure why they didn't get them to send the invitation letter. Apparently I had designed a house for her and her husband and Laszlo had done the electrical work, but I really didn't remember her face. I did a lot of house plans back then and Laszlo did a lot of electrical work and it was hard to remember each person individually. I could vaguely remember a young woman who had a baby about the same time that I had Csilla and we would sometimes see each other when we were pushing our prams. However they did remember us quite well. They had lived a few streets away from us. In any case we decided that we would help them out if we could. It wasn't a big thing for us to do and it could prove to be their only chance to come here. We sent the letter and they said that they would go to their relatives place in Sydney, they weren't even planning on coming to Melbourne. They arrived a few months later and we heard from them a couple of times. They were settling well in Sydney and were very thankful that we had helped them out. I did say to her a couple of times that I didn't think they would be able to stay on a tourist visa and that maybe they

should find out what would happen. But she
always said not to worry, that they would work
something out before their visa had expired.
They found a place to rent and started working
and seemed very happy in their new life. While
we were a bit concerned about what would
happen, we knew it was their problem to sort
out and we didn't worry about it. She was
doing babysitting and her husband was an auto
mechanic and even though they didn't have
much English they seemed to be doing quite
well.

When it got close to September and Father's
Day I started to think about what I could get as
a surprise for Laszlo. I ended up going to the
travel agent and booking a mystery flight. This
meant I paid a set fee for an airline ticket but
the destination, was a mystery – it could have
been anywhere in the country. You could ring
up the night before and find out where the
flight was to and as it turned out ours was to
Sydney. I didn't tell Laszlo where we were
going or what we were doing but I had told him
that he had to keep the day free because I had a

surprise planned for him. When I found out we were going to Sydney I called my friend and told her that we would be arriving quite early in the morning and leaving late that afternoon. Because we had been to Sydney a few times before, we had seen all the sights so I thought that we could spend the day with them and finally get to meet them after all this time. I rang to ask and they agreed. She had to baby-sit in the morning but she said her husband could pick us up at the airport. I thought that was a good idea but didn't know how we would be able to recognise him, as we couldn't remember his face! She said that he was tall and skinny and would be wearing greasy overalls, as he would be coming straight from work. He would then drop us off at their house and would go back to work again.

The night before I told Laszlo that we had to be up very early because we had to be at the airport by 7 o'clock the next morning. As we lived about one and a half hours drive from the airport this meant a very early start. We did manage to get up on time but then we realised that we had a flat tyre on the car. Laszlo had to change the tyre and we had to drive really fast to the airport and all this time he didn't even know where we were going! We just got to the airport on time to make our flight and then I told Laszlo where we were heading and what we were doing. He was really surprised and so happy. We did manage to find my friend's husband in his oil stained overalls and when we saw him we said, "Oh, so it's you!" We did recognise him and it was great to finally put a face to the voice. We had a really good time that day, it was great to catch up and it was also great to have a little break in a whole different city. They also took us back to the airport that afternoon, which was really nice of them. We had a lot of fun and Laszlo really enjoyed it as well, which made me happy that I had chosen it as a present for him.

The six months of their tourist visa soon passed and one day she rang me with some bad news. She said that they weren't allowed to stay on their tourist visa and they would have to leave because to apply for a residency visa you had to be out of the country. It turned out that their relatives in Sydney knew somebody in New Caledonia with whom they could stay with while they applied for residency. So they had to use all the money they had saved over the previous months to buy plane tickets to New Caledonia. I didn't hear from them after that because I didn't know where they were or even how to contact them. It turned out that they had to stay there for 13 months before their residency application was accepted. It was a long time to wait but it was worth it for them when they could eventually return.

When they returned to Australia they decided to move to the Sunshine Coast, as they didn't want to live in Sydney permanently. This had also always been our long-term plan as well – to move to the Gold Coast, Brisbane or the Sunshine Coast – we just knew that we didn't want to live in Melbourne for much longer. We had thought about leaving many times and had tried to make the break on many occasions, but because we were struggling financially, it had never yet been possible. In any case they soon moved up to Queensland and settled in Buderim and my friend's husband had a little garage in Caloundra. The following June we asked them if it was all right if we came up to visit them to have a look around and see what opportunities there were for us in this area. Laszlo's brother stayed in our place, to look after our girls and Jack, whilst we flew up to Maroochydore Airport and stayed for five days with my friends. She loaned us her car and we had the chance to drive around and see what was on offer. We really liked the area and we particularly liked the weather. We had come from a freezing Melbourne winter to the warmth of the Sunshine Coast; we couldn't believe that we could wear shorts and t-shirts in winter! This was the lifestyle that we had always wanted when we decided to come to Australia in the first place. After our visit we decided that we definitely wanted to move to Queensland. We headed back to Melbourne with plans to sell our house and get back to Queensland as soon as possible. We were anxious to go somewhere new where the cost of living wasn't so high. Our main problem since arriving in Melbourne had been that we could never quite get ahead financially. Laszlo's business was always up and down and while there were some good paying jobs, there were often times when very little was coming in. The lack of a fixed income made it very hard to keep on top of all our payments.

One day we had a really bad storm that was so fierce it was almost like a mini cyclone. The girls were at school and I let Jack inside and we watched the storm from the living room. There were high winds and heavy rain - it was really scary to watch. The wind took a few tiles from the roof, which worried me even more. Laszlo was at work and I didn't know what to do. Finally the storm died down and our next-door neighbour came over and asked me where the shed was. (We managed to buy a little shed earlier). I had a look and sure enough our shed was gone! I couldn't believe it. The wind had picked the shed up and taken it over to the yard of the house behind ours. All the stuff that had been in the shed was scattered all over our yard and theirs as well. It was a real disaster area. I had never seen anything like it; the shed had actually damaged our neighbour's roof before it had landed in his front garden. Fortunately we had insurance and we soon got our roof fixed and also got a new shed. This was actually a larger shed, it was the size of a garage and we decided that this one would be cemented down. I drew up a plan and we got a permit from the council to install our new and improved shed. It was much stronger and because we had more space Laszlo could finally have a workbench and somewhere to put his gym equipment.

We still had the old caravan; in fact it had come in quite handy while we were waiting to get our new shed because we could store the tools in the caravan and cover it with plastic. Although we had bought the caravan with the intention of making a business out of it with my brother, we had never actually done anything about it. I don't know if it was ever really a serious idea for them, but nothing happened in that area.

Chapter Twelve

Now that we had decided that we were definitely going to Queensland, we started trying to sell our house. Laszlo also had a plan for the caravan. He decided that he would fix it up and make it usable again and we could take it up with us and then sleep in it until we got ourselves settled. It was a good idea and a great way to save money but I didn't think it would be possible because the caravan was so old and wrecked. However Laszlo said that he could get it in good condition again. We took the caravan apart from the bottom up and Laszlo replaced every part. In fact he made the new frame much stronger than the old one. In the meantime I helped out by painting and de-rusting the top part, which was just a skeleton anyway. Laszlo had also managed to get a roll of aluminium sheeting. It was actually the proof from when they printed the Yellow Pages. One side of it was clean and shiny and the other had all the print from the Yellow Pages on it. It was interesting to see that it could be recycled for another useful purpose. Laszlo told me that this aluminium would become the shell of the caravan. He measured every little part of the caravan and then asked a sheet metal place nearby if he could use their folder and their guillotine to cut all the individual pieces that we would need. They were very nice and for the price of a carton of beer we got to use their tools. I helped him with the folding and the cutting and the other people who worked there were quite intrigued by what we were doing. The folding and cutting that we were doing was quite unusual and they couldn't work it out at all. When we told them that we were building a caravan they didn't believe us at first. The neighbours were the same; they didn't think that it would be possible to rebuild it.

Slowly but surely our little caravan took shape, we made a nice door and the top could open as well. We also had to cut new glass for the windows. They were just fixed windows, they didn't actually open. We got some chipboard for the floor and I managed to get some good second hand carpet, so when we were finished it looked great and we were very proud of what we had accomplished. Laszlo fixed the lights and soon it was ready to use. The only problem was that we didn't have a numberplate. Because it had been just a rusted shell before it couldn't be registered. What we actually did was borrow our friend's trailer that didn't have a numberplate. Laszlo then fixed it up a bit so it was roadworthy and took it to the Main Roads Department and applied to have it registered. They checked it out, declared it roadworthy and gave us a numberplate. We then used this numberplate for the caravan.

We had been trying to sell our house for quite a while. At first we decided that we wouldn't go through an agent but would try for a private sale, so we could save some money. First of all we advertised in the Sun newspaper, which was the big Melbourne paper. However they accidentally misprinted our phone number – it was almost the same but not quite. I rang the number they had put in the paper and asked the people there to pass on our phone number if anybody rang. It turned out that nobody rang so I'm not sure if anyone was interested or if the other people just didn't pass on our phone number. I rang the newspaper and they gave us another ad for free. We did get a few phone calls but nobody seemed particularly interested. I think one of the problems was that to look at the house from the outside it didn't seem that exciting, but inside it had much more potential. We had worked hard on it and Laszlo had installed both air-conditioning and heating, so that was a big selling point. We had a specially made drying cabinet, which sucked the used warm air and channelled it through this cabinet. It was great in winter, because you could put wet things in there at night and the next morning they would be dry. There were just lots of little things that you couldn't see from the outside.

Time soon moved on and we really needed to sell the house so we could make the move to Queensland. Eventually we decided that we would go through an agent and we started to get a bit more interest. It was hard though, because the house had to be kept perfectly tidy at all times just in case a potential buyer would come around. Even though quite a few people came, nobody seemed really interested and this was frustrating. Eventually we decided at the end of the Christmas school holidays we were going to move up to Queensland no matter what. We wanted the girls to start school at the beginning of the year. It turned out that some friends of ours needed a place to move, as their lease was due to expire on their rented house. We offered them our house to rent, which was a good temporary solution. As much as we wanted to sell the house and settle everything, at least this way we had money coming in to cover the mortgage payments.

I checked around with the removal companies and found one that sounded good. They had a really huge truck that could fit the contents of four average houses. This meant that the price was really cheap. Even with insurance it was really worthwhile. They gave us some boxes and we gradually started to pack everything up and got ready for the move. It wasn't much fun, as I don't enjoy packing but it had to be done. When you move you realise just how much stuff you can manage to accumulate over the years. A lot of it was stuff that I don't even use, but you just don't bother getting rid of it. At least when you move it is a good way to get rid of excess junk, even though it is also a lot of hard work. They picked our things up on Thursday and they wouldn't deliver them until the following Monday, so we had be organised with what we took with us. Luckily because we had the caravan we could take a lot of things like clothes, plates and cutlery with us. They even took plants, which was good because Laszlo had a few Bonsai.

It was strange living in our house for the last few days with everything packed around us. We were very short of money and had to be really careful with what we spent because we had to pay the movers before they left. Laszlo did a job and got paid by cheque but that didn't help because we couldn't cash the cheque at our local bank. We could only get it cashed at the branch where the account was held. As it turned out this person lived on the other side of Melbourne so on the morning the truck arrived I had to get up really early, drive for almost two hours and get the cheque cashed at that particular branch of the bank. When I got there the teller said I could have taken it to my local branch and they could have faxed the signature across to save me coming all that way. I couldn't believe it but there wasn't much I could do then. I just wish that they had told me that before I had gone all that way. She cashed the cheque and I rushed back home with the money. They had done all the packing and were just waiting for me to arrive to pay them. After the truck left we had an empty house. Everything was packed in the caravan and I was really worried about Jack. I didn't know how he would react because everything was new and strange for him. We had a Nissan Bluebird station wagon and he would have to travel in the back. We had already decided that we would stop along the way at a caravan park that catered for animals.

It was really weird to stay in the empty house for the final night. We left early the next morning. The neighbours came out to say goodbye and then it was time to leave Melbourne. We were all set to head north for our new life in Queensland.

Chapter Thirteen

We arrived in Queensland on the 21st of January 1994. Jack was really well behaved the whole trip up. We didn't have any problems with him at all. At first we stayed with my friend, but this was just until we found our feet. We didn't like to apply for the dole again but it was necessary to have some money coming in while we organised our new life.

We started looking for a house to rent almost right away. My friend had a dog, who Jack didn't get along with, so it was necessary to move as soon as possible. We found an old house in Maroochydore, which Laszlo really liked because it had a showroom in the front. He was hoping to set up a business installing alarms, intercoms and ducted vacuum systems, so we thought that the showroom would come in handy. We moved into this house, which was opposite to Maroochydore High School. It was also very close to the primary school, so that was very convenient for the kids. I saw an ad for experienced mushroom pickers while I was at the job centre, so I contacted them and got the job. This was where I worked for the next four and a half years.

It took Laszlo a while to get a full time job. He did try setting up a business at home but it didn't work out. He had met a man who wanted to be a partner in the business – he financed the equipment to begin with, which was very helpful. They worked hard, but unfortunately didn't get much business. After about three months they had to close because hardly any jobs were coming in and they weren't making any money. Laszlo's partner decided that he wanted to leave the partnership, so the business was dissolved. Eventually Laszlo found a nighttime cleaning job. We only had one car at the time so I would take it to work during the day and he would take it at night. We didn't get to see a lot of each other but it was good to have money coming in. Eventually we had to move from that house as the rent was too high and we didn't need the showroom any more when Laszlo started his cleaning job. We moved to another rented house in Maroochydore.

Meanwhile back in Melbourne the tenants had moved out of our house and it remained empty. We couldn't afford the mortgage payments without the rental income, so the bank informed us that we would have to sell. We put it in the hands of an agent and knew that we would have to make a quick sale, as we still owed a fair amount of money. Once again we found ourselves in a difficult financial position. Because we still owed money on the mortgage and because of other financial problems we weren't able to have any credit cards or borrow money. The only way that we could buy any type of major household appliance was to save up the money and pay cash. This was really frustrating sometimes, but we managed okay.

After I had been at the mushroom farm for a while we found a nighttime job cleaning buses. For the next two years we worked washing buses every night, including public holidays and even on Christmas night. I still worked at the mushroom farm and Laszlo found other odd jobs to do during the day – things like cleaning and concreting swimming pools. Eventually all our hard work paid off and we were able to repay all our debt. Finally Laszlo found work in an air-conditioning business and he could go back to working days again. Things started to pick up a bit then. After he had been working there for a while he was asked to sub-contract rather than work for wages. He did this and this was how he got back into the air-conditioning business.

My mother decided to come for a visit in November 1995 and planned to stay for three months. I hadn't seen her since the time she came to visit us in Austria, which was 8 years before. Although I really wanted to see her I was a bit nervous about having her come to stay for so long. After I had married Laszlo we hadn't actually lived in the same house, we had only lived next door to each other. As I have mentioned earlier in the story this arrangement caused quite a few problems between us, so I wasn't sure how we would manage being in the same house together for so long.

It turned out that I didn't need to worry – her whole visit was really pleasant. Mum loved every minute of her stay. She played with the kids and really made the most of her time with them. We took her to lots of different places and showed her all the sights and she enjoyed it all. I also had lots of time to sit with her and have a good chat about the past and all the things that had happened in our family. It was just amazing that we were able to communicate so well after having had some problems in the past. We even went to Melbourne to visit mine and Laszlo's brother. She went home on the 14th of February, which is Valentine's Day of course. It was very difficult to say goodbye – we cried a lot. It's always very hard when you live so far away from your family because you always think that this could be the last time you see them. It was a really pleasant experience for all of us and I was so glad she came.

In the meantime Csilla had continued to go really well with her gymnastics. She represented Queensland at the national championships in Darwin and got great results. Anita did well at school. She met a boy there and they got quite serious. After finishing high school they got married and then started working. We surprised them with a ticket to Hungary, which made us really happy. We had heard an ad on the radio where if you purchased one ticket to Europe then you got another one free, so we scraped together all our savings and bought one ticket and got the other one for free. They were away for about two months altogether. As well as going to Hungary they went to Paris, Rome and other European cities. When they came back however, Anita decided that she didn't want to live with her husband anymore and they separated. They did try to work things out for a while but in the end they decided to go their separate ways.

I continued to work at the mushroom farm for several years. While I was still working there we had a phone call from Hungary to say that Laszlo's father was very sick. He was in his nineties by then and we thought that we should go home and visit him. Because we had a business we could claim it as a business trip. The price of the tickets was quite reasonable and we took Csilla with us as well. There was actually an expo on in Hungary at the time which let us claim it as a business expense. The expo turned out to be quite interesting actually.

We really enjoyed our trip back home. Everybody was fine, which was great to see. Csilla really enjoyed all the history of Hungary. Like the rest of Europe everything there was so much older, it was fascinating for her to see things that were 1000 years old or more. We had one day in Rome on the way back that we all really enjoyed as well. The whole trip was really great and we were pleased to have gone home. It was so interesting to see the changes that had taken place in the years that we had been away. One of the first things we noticed was how many more shopping centres there were – they had sprung up like mushrooms!

Anita met a new boyfriend and eventually they decided that they would move to Sydney and start a life together there. She worked and did some study as well and had been doing very well down there. When we returned from Hungary I had some problems with the mushroom farm. They started cutting back my wages without telling me and didn't have any proper explanation when I questioned them about it. It was a bit sad to start having problems after working there for four and a half years, but when we couldn't resolve things I decided that I would leave. I was really upset at the time because I was a bit lost. Laszlo's business was doing well and he was very busy but I didn't really know what direction that I should take. Then one of our old friends suggested that I should go to TAFE and get my Australian qualification, so in 1999 I went to TAFE in Nambour and completed my certificate in drafting. I ended up coming second in the class. I was really proud of myself when I finished and received my certificate.

In the meantime we moved our business into a shed and we started manufacturing sheet metal ducts as well as installation of air conditioning systems. It started out quite slowly but it grew a lot. We started getting really busy and at one time we had 19 men working for us. Having that many staff cost us dearly though. Because some of them were taking things a bit too easy on the job we lost a lot of money. We then had to cut back drastically on staff and ended up with just two workers and a secretary. Unfortunately our debt was a concern and after a long negotiation with the taxation department we were ordered to close the business and to go into voluntary liquidation, which was very disappointing. Just before all this the lease on our shed expired and we had to find another one to lease. This added to the stress of the situation. Fortunately we had started another business and it is still going well today. We are extremely busy these days manufacturing sheet metal ducting for many different air-conditioning businesses. We restructured our business so now there is just Laszlo and I running it. I do the office work and also help Laszlo in the shed. I do insulation and the assembling of these systems. It is good to catch up financially again.

Unfortunately things with my brother and his wife have not improved. They came up to Noosa for two weeks during the Christmas/New Year period of 1999/2000 and they didn't come to see us. I found out later that they had been up and I questioned them about it. They didn't have any particular reason why they had not been in contact. I really don't know what we ever did or said to make things so unpleasant between us. If they can't tell us then we can't do anything about it. We haven't had any contact with them since that time.

After renting for six years we were finally able to afford to buy a house in Buderim in November 2000. Luckily for us it was before the recent real estate boom, which has seen property values increase so much. We got it for a good price and the value has improved quite significantly, so it was definitely a good investment.

When Csilla finished high school she enrolled at Griffith University to study Primary Education. After her first year she decided to defer for one year and have a break from study. During this year she coached gymnastics at the Maroochy Beach Gymnastics Club. Her kids were really successful and everybody loved her, so that was great for her. She had told us that if she missed her uni course then she would go back and if not then it wasn't meant to be. At the end of the year she decided to move to Sydney and apply for the same course at Sydney University. She got accepted and moved down to Sydney with Anita. She soon met a boy and Anita and their boyfriends all lived together for a while, but they now have their own places. Csilla moved closer to the university, so there was less travel for her to do. We are extremely proud of Anita and Csilla and they are both very successful with what they have done in their lives. We are trilled that they are happy in what they have chosen to do. Jack is still with us after all this time. He turned 10 this year and is still going well.

We may have had many financial struggles since arriving in Australia, but through working hard we have managed to come out on top. We read a lot of books to help us and have learned so much about how things work and the best ways to succeed in all aspects of life. We are so happy that we have just been able to buy an investment property in Brisbane. It shows that we have come such a long way since arriving here all those years ago. We hope to continue to succeed with our business and we also look forward to buying some more investment properties.

We have really changed a lot since arriving in Australia. In Hungary people tend to live their lives worrying too much about what other people think. In Australia people tend to be more accepting about letting everybody just live their own lives. They get on with doing the things that they want to do. We feel here that we are living our lives in the way that we have decided to and we aren't doing things for show. We don't care very much what other people think of what we have or what we do; we just want to be happy within ourselves. I also learned not to get involved in other people's business – just like I don't want other people to be involved in mine. With my daughters I have always tried to be supportive in whatever they decide to do. This only encourages them to do better. I am so proud of them and I don't want to interfere in their lives. We have made a lot of friends and while we are always available to them if they need our help, we have tried not to get too deeply involved with any of them. Some people, particularly Hungarians, can get extremely jealous of others and we don't like to have that kind of animosity with any of our friends. We would rather live our own lives the way we want to than feel that we have to compete with any of our friends.

Laszlo and I are both really happy that we moved to Australia. We had a hard start but we really like it here. We are friendly and happy people ourselves and so we have made friends wherever we have gone. I believe that whatever you give out you get back. I'm extremely happy with my life at this time and feel very lucky to be where I am today.

On 20th of January 2004 Laszlo's Dad past away at age 95 in Hungary. The same day we had to put Jack to sleep due to an incurable illness.

Printed in the United States
By Bookmasters